Islam and Human Rights

Significant Issues Series
Timely books presenting current CSIS research and analysis of interest to the academic, business, government, and policy communities.
Managing Editor: Roberta Howard Fauriol

The Center for Strategic and International Studies (CSIS) is a nonprofit, bipartisan public policy organization established in 1962 to provide strategic insights and practical policy solutions to decisionmakers concerned with global security. Over the years, it has grown to be one of the largest organizations of its kind, with a staff of some 200 employees, including more than 120 analysts working to address the changing dynamics of international security across the globe.

CSIS is organized around three broad program areas, which together enable it to offer truly integrated insights and solutions to the challenges of global security. First, CSIS addresses the new drivers of global security, with programs on the international financial and economic system, foreign assistance, energy security, technology, biotechnology, demographic change, the HIV/AIDS pandemic, and governance. Second, CSIS also possesses one of America's most comprehensive programs on U.S. and international security, proposing reforms to U.S. defense organization, policy, force structure, and its industrial and technology base and offering solutions to the challenges of proliferation, transnational terrorism, homeland security, and post-conflict reconstruction. Third, CSIS is the only institution of its kind with resident experts on all the world's major populated geographic regions.

CSIS was founded four decades ago by David M. Abshire and Admiral Arleigh Burke. Former U.S. senator Sam Nunn became chairman of the CSIS Board of Trustees in 1999, and since April 2000, John J. Hamre has led CSIS as president and chief executive officer.

Headquartered in downtown Washington, D.C., CSIS is a private, tax-exempt, 501(c) 3 institution.

The CSIS Press
Center for Strategic and International Studies
1800 K Street, N.W., Washington, D.C. 20006
Tel: (202) 887-0200   Fax: (202) 775-3199
E-mail : books@csis.org   Web: www.csis.org

Islam and Human Rights

Advancing a U.S.-Muslim Dialogue

EDITED BY SHIREEN T. HUNTER WITH HUMA MALIK

THE CSIS PRESS

**Center for Strategic
and International Studies**

Washington, D.C.

Significant Issues Series, Volume 27, Number 5
© 2005 by Center for Strategic and International Studies
Washington, D.C.
Printed on recycled paper in the United States of America
Cover design by Robert L. Wiser, Silver Spring, Md.
Cover photograph: © Lynsey Addario/Corbis. A young Afghan girl in a
classroom in Kabul, October 2002. After the fall of the Taliban, many
Afghan girls were able to go to school for the first time.

09 08 07 06 05   5 4 3 2 1

ISSN 0736-7136
ISBN 0-89206-471-4

Library of Congress Cataloging-in-publication Data
Islam and human rights : advancing a U.S.–Muslim dialogue / edited by Shireen T.
Hunter with Huma Malik.
     p. cm. — (Significant issues series ; v. 27. no. 5)
   Includes bibliographical references and index.
   ISBN 0-89206-471-4
1. Human rights—Religious aspects—Islam. 2. Human rights—United States. I.
Hunter, Shireen. II. Malik, Huma. III. Title. IV. Series.
  BP173.44.I854 2006
  297.2'72—dc22
                 2005009237

CONTENTS

8. CONCLUSIONS

PREFACE

In the last few years, issues related to human rights, including encouraging the democratization of Muslim societies from the Middle East to Southeast Asia, have acquired great importance in shaping the character of U.S.–Muslim relations and U.S. policy toward Muslim countries.

An important impetus behind this development has been the tragic events of September 11, 2001, which demonstrated the threatening and destructive dimensions of the rise of militant and violent groups that use a distorted interpretation of Islam to justify their actions. These events also led to a greater realization by the United States—and the West—that lack of democracy and lack of respect for human rights have been contributory factors behind the rise of militant Islam.

Consequently, in its approach toward the Muslim world the United States has emphasized the themes of promoting democracy and human rights. The efforts of the United States to establish democratic governments in Afghanistan and Iraq following military interventions there exemplify this new focus of U.S. policy. Within the Islamic world, too, both secular and more moderate and reformist Islamists have been focusing on issues related to democracy and human rights.

Certain fundamental questions, however, remain the subject of intense debate in both the United States and the Muslim world. These questions pertain to the compatibility of Islam with the concept of human rights as enshrined in the Universal Declaration of Human Rights (UDHR) and other international conventions, and pertain as well to the U.S. approach to the application of human rights standards to different countries. Some U.S. and other Western observers, as well as many secular and conservative Muslims, believe that Islam is incompatible with human rights. By contrast, other Western observers and scholars, as well as reformist Muslim thinkers and activists, maintain that a proper reading of Islamic injunctions and, more importantly, an understanding of the ethical values underpinning those injunctions shows that Islam is compatible with basic standards of human rights.

Meanwhile, secular as well as conservative and reformist Muslims harbor doubts about the seriousness of the U.S.—and Western—commitment to the cause of democracy and human rights. They believe that the United States applies human rights' standards selectively, whenever and wherever it serves U.S. strategic and economic interests. Irrespective of their validity, these charges nevertheless constitute part of the context of U.S.–Muslim relations as they pertain to the issue of human rights.

Given the importance of this issue in overall U.S.–Muslim relations, the CSIS Islam Program held a conference in fall 2004 entitled "Human Rights: How to Advance U.S.–Muslim Dialogue." The conference brought together Muslim and U.S. scholars who are dealing with these issues, as well as representatives of the U.S. government, the broader policymaking community, and nongovernmental organizations active in the human rights field. This volume is the result of that conference.

The conference was made possible by a generous grant from the Rockfeller Brothers Fund and additional support from the Friedrich Ebert Foundation and the LUSO-American Foundation. Huma Malik and I wish, therefore, to express the appreciation of CSIS and ourselves for their support. We also would like to thank the contributors to this volume for their valuable insights.

I hope that this volume will help lead to a greater understanding of the relationship between Islam and human rights within the broader context of the evolving notions of human rights and, moreover, will help advance a U.S.–Muslim dialogue on this issue of vital importance and thus help promote the cause of human rights in the Muslim world and globally.

Shireen T. Hunter
Director, Islam Program
Center for Strategic and International Studies
Washington, D.C.

CHAPTER ONE

INTRODUCTION

Shireen T. Hunter

Among the factors affecting the state of relations between the United States, and the West in general, and the Muslim world, the issue of human rights has acquired greater significance in the post-Soviet era, particularly in the last few years. Freed from the security constraints of the Cold War, the United States and other Western countries have come to put more emphasis on human rights as an important factor in shaping their approach toward Muslim countries.

However, because new threats and challenges have emerged—notably the spread of a more violent version of Islamist extremism that poses a threat to Western interests and, in some cases, security—the age-old tension between ideals and interests and the dilemma of how to reconcile the guaranteeing of respect for human rights with securing more tangible strategic and economic interests have not disappeared. Consequently, the application of human rights standards by the United States and other Western countries to different states in the Muslim world has remained uneven. Countries deemed important for the protection and advancement of U.S. and Western interests have been dealt with more leniently in matters relating to human rights than have countries viewed as hostile to the United States and the West.

This situation, in turn, has intensified the feeling among a large segment of Muslim populations that the United States and Western nations are not strongly committed to the cause of human rights in the Muslim world and that they apply a double standard in dealing with different countries.

Beyond these policy-related issues, there is a more fundamental debate between the United States and the West, on the one hand, and the Muslim world, on the other. This debate concerns the universality of the concept of human rights as developed in the West and enshrined in the Universal Declaration of Human Rights (UDHR) and other human rights conventions developed in the following decades. Interestingly, this issue is also divisive both within the Muslim world and in the United States. In the Muslim world, secularized Muslims tend to subscribe to the idea of the universal validity of the UDHR, while the more religious-minded have a more relativist view of its validity. In other words, the latter subscribe to the UDHR to the extent that it does not conflict with their Islamic religious values and notions of right and wrong. In the United States and some other Western countries, a non-negligible portion of the populations also view as invalid those notions of human rights that conflict with their religious beliefs and injunctions. Meanwhile, a considerable body of opinion in the Muslim world maintains that Islamic religious and ethical systems are inherently incompatible with Western notions of human rights.

In short, differences regarding various dimensions of the human rights debate constitute an important part of the broader context of U.S. and Western relations with the Muslim world and thus require special efforts to resolve them and reach common ground for the promotion of human rights in the Muslim world and globally.

Rather than merely focusing on Islamic exceptionalism, a first step in this direction is to put the current debate between the Muslim world and the United States, and the West, into the broader context of the historical evolution of the concept of human rights, notably their nature, range, source, and scope of applicability. This is important in advancing a U.S.–Muslim dialogue on this issue for the ultimate purpose of promoting respect for human rights in the Muslim world and globally.

UNIVERSALITY VERSUS RELATIVITY

Since ancient times, the fundamental question that has been asked in this regard has been the following: Are there certain ethical values that transcend boundaries of specific cultures and confer certain inalienable rights on people by virtue of their being human; or are ethical values—and the rights ensuing from them—culture-based and hence relative?

Although glimpses of this debate can be seen in most ancient cultures, its most concrete cases are found in ancient Greece and Rome.[1] The Greek historian Herodotus, after observing the customs of various people and their ethical basis, concluded that there was no ethical system with universal application.[2] The Sophists, too, did not believe in universal ethics and, hence, rights with universal application. Rather, they maintained that notions of goodness and justice were relative to the customs of each society and were often offered to disguise the interests of the stronger.

The Stoics, by contrast, building on the ideas of Socrates and Plato, believed in universal ethical values and hence rights with universal application.[3] In Rome, Cicero, who was deeply influenced by Greek thought, including the Stoics, argued that "there is in fact a true law ... namely right reason which in accordance with nature applies to all men." He called this law *ius naturales* (natural law) and distinguished it from *ius gentium* (laws of nations). Cicero considered the idea that everything is just by virtue of laws or customs to be foolish since the laws could have been enacted by tyrants.[4]

These notions of an ethical system giving rise to rights that have universal application and that transcend cultural boundaries were largely, but not completely, forgotten for many centuries only to reappear with a renewed force in the eighteenth century. Since then, there has been considerable movement toward the recognition that certain ethical values underpinning the notion that human beings have certain inalienable rights have universal validity. The UDHR is the culmination of this movement. As noted earlier, however, the universality-versus-relativity debate has not yet been resolved. Moreover, as often as not, cultural and/or religious differences have been used by repressive governments to deny the rights of their people.

SOURCE OF RIGHTS: DIVINE VERSUS SECULAR

Another dividing line in the debate about human rights that has significant implications for the differences between Muslim countries and the United States and the West is the question of the source of rights, namely, whether rights are conferred on human beings by God or whether they exist in nature and can be discovered by the application of reason. Another relevant issue is whether human beings can overlook divine proscriptions of certain types of behavior in the name of inalienable human rights, including freedom of choice. Although this dichotomy is observed most clearly today in Muslim societies, elements of it are observable in the United States and, to a much lesser extent, in Europe as well.

Yet many of the rights recognized in the natural law theory of rights are also granted by most religious systems, notably the three monotheistic religions. Indeed, in regard to economic and social rights, religiously based rights are more advanced than those recognized in the eighteenth and nineteenth centuries' version of rights. In Islam in particular, the concept of social and economic justice and of the responsibility of the community to provide for its more vulnerable members is highly important.

RANGE AND HIERARCHY OF RIGHTS

The concept of what constitutes basic human rights has steadily expanded since the eighteenth century. This has largely resulted from technological and scientific developments changing agrarian societies into industrial ones and the social and political consequences of that transformation. Initially, the focus was on civil and political rights, plus the rights of property owners. Following the industrial revolution and the emergence of vast urban working classes, the focus shifted to the development of ideologies emphasizing the securing of social and economic rights. However, even after the adoption of the UDHR, which includes both sets of rights, there was a gap between the advanced industrialized states and the less developed countries on the relative importance of these two sets of rights. The latter thought that the UDHR had not paid enough attention to social and economic rights, and they pushed for new legislation that resulted in the adoption of the United Nation's International Covenant on Economic, Social and Cultural Rights in December 1966. In the context of political rights, too, developing countries emphasized the right to self-determination.

Today, although all agree that both sets of rights—civil-political and social-economic—are essential and must be respected, there is still no agreement on their relative importance. Many less-developed countries, including Muslim countries, emphasize social and economic rights at the expense of civil and political rights. This approach, however, is often a device to deny their people their civil and political rights. Meanwhile, the United States and other Western countries generally emphasize civil and political rights. This position, too, is flawed because very poor and illiterate people often are neither aware of their civil and political rights nor capable of acquiring them.

Yet selective approaches to rights persist and are a source of division between the United States and the Muslim world. Meanwhile, paradoxically, this selective approach is bringing U.S. positions on certain issues closer to those of Muslim countries.

APPLICABILITY: HUMAN RIGHTS FOR WHOM?

The issue of who is entitled to benefit from basic rights has also been the subject of debate since ancient times. Historically, the applicability of rights has had severe limits and its scope has enlarged gradually. For example, slaves, women, foreigners, followers of certain religions, and propertyless classes were deprived of all or some rights. Colonial peoples also were deprived of certain rights, notably that of self-determination. Even today, there are groups that because of race, religion, gender, and other characteristics are deprived of certain basic rights.

The Muslim world contains glaring cases of discrimination against women and certain religious minorities. Whether Islam is responsible for this situation or whether particular governments misuse Islam to justify these discriminatory practices is the subject of intense debate both in the West and in the Muslim world. Cases concerning the status of women and religious minorities also represent areas of tension between the United States and the Muslim world in the broader context of the human rights debate.

IDEALS VERSUS INTERESTS

Another major issue in the context of the human rights debate has been how to reconcile the goal of spreading respect for basic human rights with safeguarding other state interests. At times, the promotion of the cause of human rights has served other state interests. But more often these two objectives have tended to clash. This has resulted in the selective application of human rights standards and raised the issue of double standards in this regard. These dilemmas remain unresolved.

In sum, more than half a century after the adoption of the UDHR, debate about various dimensions of human rights continues.

This situation therefore demands that the current differences between the United States and the West and the Muslim world in regard to human rights be looked at in the broader context of the evolution of the human rights debate, while also taking into account a number of important issues specific to the Muslim world. That is precisely what this volume aims to do.

In the following chapters, Ann Elizabeth Mayer (chapter 2) analyses the present state of the debate between the United States and the Muslim world within the broader context of the evolving concepts of human rights. Next, Khalid Abou Al Fadl (chapter 3) addresses the question of whether there is an Islamic view of human rights, thus helping to identify areas of convergence and divergence between an Islamic concept of human rights and the concepts embodied in the UDHR and other international conventions. Recep Senturk (chapter 4) deals with the question of minority rights in Islam, drawing especially but not exclusively on the Ottoman experience; he argues that the universalist school of thought in Islam as first formulated by Abu Hanifa (699–767 CE) advocates equal rights for all human beings regardless of their inherited and innate qualities such as race, religion, ethnicity, and class. Riffat Hassan (chapter 5) addresses the issue of gender in Islam and demonstrates how treatment of women in the Muslim world is against Islam's normative teachings. Saad Eddin Ibrahim (chapter 6) looks at the various reasons behind the poor record of human rights in Muslim countries and places in their proper context those reasons deriving from certain interpretations of Islam. Finally, Robert Pastor (chapter 7) addresses the issue of U.S. policy on human rights and democracy and the challenge of reconciling ideals and interests.

The concluding chapter brings together the insights provided by the contributors and identifies possible ways to both promote progressive thinking in the Muslim world on human rights-related issues and advance the dialogue between the United States and the Muslim world.

Notes

1. For the full discussion of these debates, see Micheline R. Ishay, *The History of Human Rights: From Ancient Times to the Globalization Era* (Berkeley: University of California Press, 2004), 21–22, 25–26.

2. Ibid., 16.

3. Ibid., 23–24.

4. Ibid., 24–25.

CHAPTER TWO

EVOLVING CONCEPTS OF HUMAN RIGHTS

Ann Elizabeth Mayer

In her Nobel lecture on December 10, 2003, the Iranian attorney Shirin Ebadi called for looking back 2,500 years to ancient Persia's ruler Cyrus the Great (580–529 BC), advising her audience that he had produced one of the most important documents in the history of human rights. She was referring to the famous "Cyrus cylinder," a tablet on which the ruler had proclaimed his enlightened and magnanimous policies for treating the inhabitants of conquered Babylon.[1] Although it does not use the language of human rights, the ancient cylinder comprises ideas that are related to modern concepts of rights—for example, the policy of respecting different religious beliefs, presaging the right to freedom of religion. Members of other cultural traditions could similarly locate various ancient and medieval precursors of human rights in their respective heritages.

However ancient its underlying concepts, the term "human rights" has only relatively recently come into common usage. With the rise of the powerful modern nation-state in the eighteenth-century, discussions of human rights emerged. As one scholar has noted, "Society, which once protected a person's dignity and provided a place in the world, now appears in the form of the modern state, the modern economy, and the modern city, as an oppressive, alien power that assaults people's dignity."[2] Not surprisingly, it was in the course of revolutions against the rulers of powerful states, Britain and France, that one saw influential rights formulations being articulated, such as the 1776 American Declaration of Independence and the 1789 French Declaration of the Rights of Man and of the Citizen. Both of these declarations were reactions to misgovernment, and both reflected the influence of

European Enlightenment ideas. In that era European theorists had posited that, whether as individuals or as groups, people needed guarantees against state coercion and arbitrary violence and protections to stop governments from restricting their freedom.

As forms of capitalism untrammeled by concerns for human suffering spread in the wake of the Industrial Revolution, nineteenth-century socialist thought responded. Seeking to address acute economic exploitation and the vast gap between the affluent and the poor that characterized laissez-faire capitalist systems, European socialists produced formulas aimed at ameliorating the plight of working people and guaranteeing all persons the requisites of a decent life. Rather than concerning themselves with finding ways to keep the state from infringing upon individuals' freedoms, socialist thinkers conceived that states had social welfare responsibilities. They elaborated rights like the right to work and to join trade unions and the right to an adequate standard of living.

By the second half of the twentieth century, people in developing countries—the Global South—were in a position to voice demands for solutions to their shared problems. Concerned with the vast gulf separating conditions in rich countries from those in poor ones, with the aftereffects of European imperialism, and with difficulties in the development process, representatives of the Global South called for recognizing rights that would further their demands for the redistribution of wealth, for self-determination, for sharing scientific and technical advances, and for other goals tied to their situation.

By the time that the United Nations was founded in the wake of World War II, it was clear that the idea of human rights in the abstract had won widespread acceptance—without, however, there being a consensus on its cultural or philosophical underpinnings. After protracted debates on the Universal Declaration of Human Rights (UDHR), unresolved questions still remained on basic issues such as how human rights were determined, whether they were a function of culture or ideology, or whether they were products of a regional or global consensus.

Nonetheless, most would concur that "human rights" as presently understood have certain basic characteristics. Among them: human rights involve claims by individuals or groups against people or institutions that are made with the aim of realizing valued goals or capabilities, comprising "fundamental" as distinct from "nonessential" claims. Human rights are also quintessentially general or universal in character, extending to every person on earth, without discrimination, simply for being human. Human rights claims can range from the justiciable to the merely aspirational. They partake of both the legal and the moral orders. Human rights can be used as standards for judging the legitimacy of laws and traditions.[3] Ronald Dworkin has famously proposed that human rights are trumps, overriding other competing policy considerations,[4] and this principle has won wide currency.

THE SIGNIFICANCE OF INCORPORATING HUMAN RIGHTS IN THE UN SYSTEM

Many ideas that anticipate our modern concepts of human rights were elaborated within the contexts of specific civilizational heritages, often in the form of enumerations of duties that individuals owed to others and to the community. A momentous shift occurred with the United Nations project of setting forth one standardized set of human rights as part of international law. The issuance of the 1948 Universal Declaration of Human Rights was a developmental milestone, calling for universality and placing supporters of particularistic standards on the defensive.[5] Of course, the UDHR did not end the disputes among philosophers, ethicists, theologians, and other thinkers on human rights. But it did mean that provisions in UN declarations and treaties began to take center stage.

When it comes to the readily recognizable antecedents of the UN formulations of civil and political rights, the so-called negative or first-generation rights that place limits on actions of governments, one sees precursors in eighteenth-century European thought. Similarly, the most influential precedents for the UN statements of economic and social rights, the so-called positive or second-generation rights, that require states to provide for people's basic needs, came from European socialist thought of the nineteenth century.[6] A point that is often missed is that the UDHR comprises both first- and second-generation rights, treating both as if they were equally vital, a perspective that the United States has never accepted.

The charge is often made that the concepts in the UDHR are "Western." True—when the UN was founded, African and Asian countries were grossly underrepresented. However, a review of the record shows that representatives of many cultures were consulted in the preliminary discussions leading up to the actual work on the UDHR. In the UN sessions where the content of the UDHR was debated, inputs came from countries from all parts of the world, including a number of smaller countries, and the Asian input was considerable.[7]

Reaching a consensus on the text of the proposed UDHR proved difficult. Among other things, there was contention about whether human rights were religious in nature and how the answer to that question should affect the text of the UDHR. Due to the inability to achieve consensus on this point, the issue had to be avoided in the final document. But the disagreements did not necessarily reflect an East-West divide. Peng-chun Chang of China, one of the main drafters, did not think that the reasons why the delegations agreed were as important as what they agreed to. He believed that it was possible to reach an overlapping consensus on the contents of the declaration even while starting from different cultural and religious premises. Rejecting the stereotyping of the East or the West as cultural monoliths, each with its own uniform culture, he did not envisage East-West clashes over competing value systems. His view was that "culturally, there are many 'Easts' and many 'Wests'; and they are by no means all necessarily irreconcilable."[8]

Despite disagreements over various provisions of the UDHR, when it came to the crucial General Assembly vote in 1948 UN members generally backed the declaration. No country voted against the UDHR, and those abstaining from the vote were mostly from the Communist bloc, Saudi Arabia being the only Muslim country to abstain. Voting reflected the politics of the moment rather than definitive "civilizational" stances. Thus, South Africa, one of the 1948 abstainers, has with the overthrow of the apartheid regime emerged as one of the countries most committed to upholding international human rights.

Of course, many Muslim countries did not have a chance to express their opinions because they were not yet members of the United Nations. In general, however, the significant contributions made by representatives of Muslim countries to the two main human rights covenants and other instruments would indicate that they found human rights ideas congenial.[9]

Do UN votes on documents like the UDHR actually signify meaningful endorsements of human rights ideas? Not necessarily. One needs to bear in mind that considerable hypocrisy could be involved, as Richard Falk has observed.[10] States may profess support for standards when they have no intention of upgrading their laws to meet them. Many countries may have voted in favor of the UDHR without anticipating that the declaration would subsequently go on to achieve such prestige and influence that noncompliance would cause acute embarrassment. For example, one of the central ideas of the UDHR is the equality of all human beings, a principle that in 1948 was generally honored in the breach rather than in observance. Because countries continued discriminating against women, against racial and religious groups, against disfavored ethnicities and indigenous peoples, and/or against the colonized peoples whom they ruled, their voting in favor of the UDHR hardly signaled a meaningful commitment to the right to equality.

With the UN being entrusted with the mission of formulating human rights, decisions by national governments now play a major role in controlling the evolution of international law. Various nongovernmental organizations (NGOs) do seek a voice in UN human rights debates, but the prominence of governmental representatives injects a strongly political component into the human rights system. For example, although "Islamic" positions on rights may be adumbrated in UN forums, these first and foremost reflect the current policies and interests of the various national governments involved.

Under UN auspices, international human rights law has vastly expanded, with new principles being set forth in a long series of UN declarations and treaties.[11] New frontiers have been regularly opened as concepts of human rights keep expanding. But there has also been resistance to such expansion. One tendency has been to break down the original "human" category into more specific subcategories, such as women, children, the disabled, or indigenous peoples, on the theory that certain groups require protections geared to their specific situations. Using ideas developed in various national systems and especially in Europe,[12] an intense controversy has raged at the UN over whether international law needs to expand to treat homosexuals as a new category requiring special protections. Where the creation of the new subcategories threatens an established patriarchal order or challenges traditional rules on sexual morality, religious conservatives have mobilized to combat proposals for expanding human rights; notably, this has occurred both in Muslim countries and in the United States, a rare Organization of Economic Cooperation and Development (OECD) country where religiosity remains a politically potent force.

RECENT CHALLENGES TO UNIVERSALISM

Notwithstanding the fact that the UDHR was not identified with a particular culture or religious view, a mounting chorus of objections, purportedly grounded in specific cultures and specific religions, has recently been raised to it as well as other UN documents. Especially since the mid-1980s, claims have been made that international human rights law is imbued with values that are essentially Western and are incompatible with non-Western traditions. Official claims regarding how "Asian values" or Islamic tradition may require distinctive approaches to human rights have been put forward as ways to challenge the ideal of the universality of human rights that was central to the original UN system.

Taking the position that Muslims must have their own separate version of human rights, the Organization of the Islamic Conference (OIC) issued its 1990 Cairo Declaration on Human Rights in Islam, which reflected many reactionary ideas promoted by governments in countries like Iran and Saudi Arabia. Because its provisions seriously dilute and sometimes eliminate the protections afforded under international law, the declaration is tantamount to a claim that Islam stands in the way of accepting international human rights.[13] In addition to the OIC effort, a number of Muslim countries—not coincidentally ones with deplorable human rights records—have appealed to Islamic particularism in an effort to discredit critiques of their human rights records.[14] In other publications I have analyzed these claims and have pointed out why they are problematic.[15]

These attempts to destabilize the international consensus supporting human rights have been deplored by human rights activists and NGOs from around the globe whose shared belief in universality creates a bridge linking Western human rights activists with their counterparts in other regions. The ideas of Iranian Nobel laureate Shirin Ebadi, an attorney who is a vigorous supporter of international human rights law, exemplify the positions that human rights activists within Muslim countries typically espouse. She has been outspoken in her assertions that support for international human rights is perfectly congruent with fidelity to Islamic culture. Her great popularity in Iran shows that she is not alone in thinking this way. Thus, the notion that Islam by itself blocks the acceptance of UN standards is shown to be misguided; that there are many "Islams" needs to be kept in mind.

The sharp contrast between Shirin Ebadi's commitment to universality and the Iranian regime's insistence on upholding Islamic particularism reminds one of the gulfs that may separate governmental and popular attitudes on human rights questions. In Ebadi's case, the gap between her beliefs and those of Iran's hard-line clerics is reflective of a much wider popular rejection of Iranian governmental policies of using Islam as a pretext for denying human rights. In a brief democratic experiment before the rigged elections of 2004, Iranians were twice allowed a chance to elect a president, Mohammed Khatami, who represented their aspirations to enjoy human rights and democracy, and they gave him overwhelming endorsements.

In many cases, however, ascertaining popular attitudes toward human rights in the Muslim world is more complicated. Given the lack of democracy in typical Muslim Middle Eastern countries, it may be hard or even impossible for disenfranchised citizens in that region to register exactly what they want in the way of human rights.

THE UNITED STATES AND MUSLIM COUNTRIES: LAGGING BEHIND INTERNATIONAL HUMAN RIGHTS STANDARDS

By the end of the twentieth century, the corpus of UN-sponsored human rights had vastly expanded. However, human rights ideas had only unevenly and incompletely penetrated many national legal systems. Systems in the United States and Muslim countries were among those lagging behind as human rights concepts continued to evolve. Both the U.S. government and governments of Muslim countries have had tense relationships with the United Nations human rights system, among other things because of their shared disinclination to implement UN standards domestically and their policy of only selectively endorsing rights precepts. Because the United States has elected to present itself as a vigorous champion of human rights on the international scene and to criticize Muslim countries' poor human rights performance, Muslims focus on the spotty and uneven U.S. record in the human rights domain, a record that harms U.S. credibility. Thus, in her Nobel acceptance speech, without referring to countries by name, Ebadi spoke critically of both repression carried out under an Islamic rubric and the United States' failure to uphold international human rights law.

One problematic aspect of the U.S. record is that U.S. law and public opinion have continued to exalt the short list of first-generation rights that one sees in the United States Constitution, the oldest constitution still in force.[16] A recent study discusses how, in contrast to other centers of Enlightenment thought like Britain and France, the United States has continued to uphold eighteenth-century ideas.[17] It is no coincidence that the First Amendment, traditionally accorded special solicitude by U.S. judges, protects freedom of speech and prohibits the establishment of religion, typical Enlightenment concerns, whereas no U.S. constitutional provisions protect the rights of children or indigenous peoples and no guarantees are afforded for rights to housing, food, access to health care, education, social security, or other basic necessities.[18]

Due to the current health care and health insurance crisis, U.S. public opinion may be ready for a change; the popular opinion seems to be moving in the direction of saying that access to health care should be considered a right. While remaining anchored in eighteenth-century traditions, to whatever extent U.S. ideas of rights have evolved can be traced to Americans' responses to specific domestic crises more than to responses to international human rights law.[19] Thus, the United States has often stood to one side as human rights ideas have moved ahead in the UN system, even winding up as the one country other than Somalia to refuse to ratify the 1989 Convention on the Rights of the Child.

The yawning gap between U.S. law and international human rights law has begun to trouble liberal members of the United States Supreme Court, who in some recent cases and in public statements have called for courts to take into account evolving human rights concepts as well as the human rights standards in force in other Western democracies.[20] The prospect that the Supreme Court might in future be guided by international human rights standards has provoked hostile reactions in

Congress, prompting efforts in November 2003 to discourage the Supreme Court from referring to international law via the introduction of the so-called Constitutional Preservation Resolution, which aimed to reinforce U.S. isolation and keep external human rights developments from infiltrating the U.S. legal system.[21]

Where equality is concerned, the U.S. orientation toward eighteenth-century ideas, where equality was a restricted concept, has been one factor impeding U.S. rights concepts from keeping pace with the evolution of international human rights law. The principle of equality in rights is an idea that has never been set forth in the Constitution. ("Equal protection" is a different principle.) Indeed, via the 1982 defeat of the proposed Equal Rights Amendment and the United States' refusal to ratify the 1981 Women's Convention, the basic international treaty upholding women's right to equality, the United States has shown itself unwilling to adjust to one of the most basic modern human rights concepts. The Women's Convention—adopted by the UN General Assembly in 1979 and officially titled the Convention on the Elimination of All Forms of Discrimination against Women (CEDAW)—symbolized how far international human rights had evolved from the outset of the UN system, when countries had given only lip service to women's equality, to a stage where it was recognized that women's rights were "unassailable, integral and indivisible elements of the universal human rights" and that the elimination of any form of gender discrimination was an overriding goal.[22]

Significantly, the United States, which did not ratify the convention when it went into force in 1981, and Muslim countries, which either did not ratify it or ratified it subject to major reservations, turned out to have similar difficulties in adjusting to the idea that women's rights were human rights warranting protection.

DISPARATE PRIORITIES IN THE UNITED STATES AND MUSLIM COUNTRIES

In some areas, U.S. policies have differed sharply from their counterparts in Muslim countries. Despite the general U.S. estrangement from the UN human rights system, many U.S. foreign policy initiatives since the presidency of Jimmy Carter have been directed at promoting a short menu of civil and political rights, concerns for religious freedom and the rights of religious minorities ranking particularly high among these. A perfect example is the establishment in 1997 of the U.S. Office of International Religious Freedom, which has the mission of promoting religious freedom as a core objective of U.S. foreign policy.[23] The office in 2003 proclaimed that

> a core American value and a cornerstone of democracy, religious freedom is a central tenet of United States foreign policy. As President Bush has repeatedly affirmed, religious freedom is a key component of U.S. efforts to ensure security, protect stability, and promote liberty.[24]

In contrast, priorities in Muslim countries are commonly very different, with the consequence that U.S. human rights policies may exacerbate tensions with both governments and peoples in the Muslim world. In the area of religious freedom there is a direct conflict between a human right that is especially esteemed and actively promoted in the U.S. tradition and the practices found in Muslim countries, where sharply circumscribed religious freedoms are the norm. Governments of Muslim countries often promote an official version of Islam as part of the state ideology, treating religious dissent as dangerous and even treasonous. This is true both in a self-professed Islamic state like Iran, where the Constitution in Article 12 expressly endorses Twelver Shi'ism as the official religion, and in countries like Turkey that may be classified as "secular" but where in practice one version of Islam is sponsored, an Islam that dovetails with state policies. Depending on whether they accept the version of Islam promoted by the government or adhere to a disfavored version of the religion, Muslims often face religious persecution and discrimination; indeed, dissenting Muslims may suffer harsher discrimination than do members of non-Muslim minority communities living in the same Muslim countries. However, discriminatory treatment of non-Muslims is also common.[25]

U.S. support for religious freedom in Muslim countries courts a popular backlash. One factor is the history of European colonialism, during which colonial powers opened the door to Christian missionaries and sought to exploit religious divisions, with favor being shown to non-Muslim minorities. U.S. pressures on issues of religious freedom, which may include freedom for Christian missionary activities and enhancing protections for non-Muslim minorities, are therefore readily associated with policies pursued by former colonial rulers.

In Muslim countries, bitter memories of European rule mean that a very different right typically strikes people as being of overwhelming importance—the right of self-determination.[26] There is widespread congruence between public opinion and governmental stances regarding the high priority to be accorded to this right.

Not surprisingly, this right was not set forth in the Universal Declaration of Human Rights. The UDHR was composed before the overthrow of European colonial rule that during the next decades gave African and Asian countries their powerful voice in the UN, enabling them to ensure that international human rights law reflected their specific interests. Showing the priority accorded to self-determination by the UN's African and Asian members, it is the first human right stipulated in the very first article of the 1966 International Covenant on Civil and Political Rights (ICCPR). The striking disparity between the UDHR and the 1966 ICCPR illustrates how within the space of only two decades human rights concepts had evolved in the UN system. The great store that people in Muslim countries place in the right of self-determination correlates closely with Muslims' preoccupation with Palestinians' failure after decades of struggle to establish an independent state.[27] U.S. positions on the Palestinian issue mean that Muslims view the United States as underrating the right of self-determination.

The right of self-determination, which includes dimensions allowing it to be seen as part of civil and political rights, is usually classed with the so-called third-generation, or solidarity, rights. These comprise rights such as the right to development, to sovereignty over natural resources, to participate in the common heritage of mankind, to peace, to a healthy and sustainable environment, and to humanitarian disaster relief. These rights, prefigured in Article 28 of the UDHR— "everyone is entitled to a social and international order in which the rights set forth in this declaration can be fully realized"—were developed in the latter half of the twentieth century, and many are closely linked to major concerns of developing countries. Concepts of third-generation rights enjoy little U.S. support.

A variety of recent statements evince Muslims' continuing preoccupation with the right of self-determination. Documents from the Arab world, whether emanating from human rights activists or from officialdom, emphasize this right.

An illustration can be found in the 1994 Arab Charter on Human Rights composed by the Council of the League of Arab States, which affirms in its very first section, Part I, Article 1(a), that all peoples have the right of self-determination.[28] Reflecting civil society perspectives, the 1999 Casablanca Declaration, which was adopted by the First International Conference of the Arab Human Rights Movement, called for "the due respect of human rights—most notably the right to self-determination," and proclaimed that

> the Conference declares its full support for the right of the Palestinian people to self-determination and to establish their independent state on their occupied national soil. . . . The rights of the Palestinian people are the proper standard to measure the consistency of international positions towards a just peace and human rights. The Arab human rights movement will apply this standard in its relations with the different international organizations and actors.[29]

Islamic sources may also be read to confirm the right to self-determination, even though Islam was not traditionally interpreted as stipulating a right to national self-determination.[30] The 1990 Cairo Declaration on Human Rights in Islam treats self-determination as an Islamic rights idea in Article 11 (b):

> Colonialism of all types being one of the most evil forms of enslavement is totally prohibited. Peoples suffering from colonialism have the full right to freedom and self-determination. It is the duty of all States and peoples to support the struggle of colonized peoples for the liquidation of all forms of [sic] and occupation.[31]

However, notwithstanding the strong support for Palestinians' rights, some in the Arab world question if the focus on this issue—a focus often encouraged by governments—has distracted people from trying to remedy the major rights deficits within their own societies.

Signaling a growing disposition to challenge the preoccupation with self-determination, participants in a June 2004 conference of more than 100 Arab intellectuals and politicians issued the Doha Declaration for Democracy and Reform. Among the statements in the declaration was a challenge to the prioritization of the Palestinian issue over the cause of democratization:

Hiding behind the necessity to resolve the Palestinian question before implementing political reform is obstructive and unacceptable. Historical experience has proven beyond a doubt that liberation movements throughout the world and democratic reform movements which grant people their freedom of expression are the best way to liberate the land and the nation. Autocratic regimes are unable or unwilling to deal seriously with outside threats and hegemonic designs. There is ample evidence that these same regimes sometimes are ready to surrender their sovereignty to ensure their own survival.[32]

This could signal the beginning of disseminating concern for an expanded range of human rights.

HOW U.S. POLICIES RELATE TO ATTITUDES IN MUSLIM COUNTRIES

In Muslim societies, government officials may differ from the people regarding many rights. For example, having endured corrupt courts and brutal criminal justice systems, people hunger for the rule of law and demand safeguards for the rights of the criminal accused. Suffering under regimes where rulers brutally repress dissent and crush independent associations, people demand the right to express critical opinions and to set up independent associations and political parties. People generally aspire to have democratized political systems where they can hold governments accountable. Many women chafe under the discriminatory treatment that they endure and aspire to greater freedoms and expanded opportunities, which government policies may deny them. Believers, whether Muslim or non-Muslim, may feel oppressed by governmental efforts to monopolize religion and to penalize those who do not defer to the state-approved orthodoxy. Thus, the prospect of expanded civil and political rights, vehemently resisted by most governments, has potent appeal at the popular level, opening the way to a favorable reception of U.S. demands for adherence to civil and political rights.

Yet, far from building bridges to restive populations, U.S. criticisms of Muslim countries' shortcomings in the area of civil and political rights may be advanced in a heavy- handed or insensitive manner that alienates Muslims. Perceptions of U.S. indifference to the Palestinian cause mean that the U.S. pattern of lecturing Muslim countries on human rights is met with resentment and cynicism. Thus, for example, the 1999 Casablanca Declaration "affirms that the Arab world is still suffering from the opportunistic, political and propagandist use of human rights by some major powers as evidenced by the double-standards employed by such powers, most notably the United States of America."[33]

The U.S. military intervention and occupation of Iraq, justified on the basis of bringing democracy to the Iraqi people and advancing their human rights, has been viewed differently by the Middle Eastern public and intellectuals. Public opinion surveys in a variety of Arab countries have indicated pervasive condemnation of U.S. Middle East policy, condemnation of the invasion of Iraq being added to the existing grievances over U.S. policies affecting Palestinians.[34]

Rashid Khalidi has suggested that by occupying Iraq, the United States effectively assumed the role formerly played by European colonial powers in a region where colonial occupiers are still bitterly resented.[35] Charges are frequently being made that the United States now displays characteristics of other imperial powers.[36] Meanwhile, popular anger over the U.S. invasion of Iraq has been a factor in Arab governments' resistance to Western calls for international intervention to deal with the massive humanitarian crisis in Darfur.[37]

Still, even though the credibility of official U.S. human rights advocacy has been weakened, in some areas Muslims' may concur with certain U.S. policies regarding human rights. For example, as the U.S. administration embraces conservative religious values, distancing U.S. policies from international standards on women's human rights, U.S. positions are moving closer to those of conservative Muslim countries that are opposed to women's equality, a fact that has been applauded by the OIC.[38] The Bush administration and various OIC states are also brought together by shared beliefs in the need to uphold traditional patriarchal institutions and restraints on sexuality.[39]

Such alliances may not be stable, however. In elevating concerns for preserving the family above concerns about women's rights, conservative forces in the United States are building bridges to Muslim conservatives at a time when powerful historical trends and the demonstrable appeal of women's international human rights are challenging the hold of conservative doctrines. The United States is effectively allying itself with the forces resisting the ongoing evolution of Islamic thought in the direction of embracing women's equality and promoting greater congruence with modern developments in international human rights.

CONCLUSION

Concepts of human rights have evolved dramatically since 1948. The United States and Muslim countries have uneven patterns of reacting to recent developments. For example, one sees that the United States still relies heavily on eighteenth-century priorities to determine which rights matter and that it has resisted the more recently evolved second- and third-generation ideas about human rights. In Muslim countries, in contrast, concepts of human rights have evolved in relation to recent political experiences, resulting in a particularly strong emphasis on the right of self-determination, a third-generation right that the United States stands accused of blatantly disregarding. However, in some other respects, one notes similarities. For example, at the governmental level, both U.S. and Muslim countries' philosophies posit that international human rights law is not necessarily binding and that it can be trumped by domestic traditions and laws—particularly ones tied to religious values and morality. The result is that domestic standards act as a drag, slowing down adjustments to evolving human rights concepts. However, one also sees some signs of pressures that could lead to changes in the direction of embracing broader spectrums of international human rights; the human rights situations in the United States and in Muslim countries are fraught with tensions that could presage further evolution in rights concepts.

Notes

[1] For one translation of the cylinder, see Vohuman.org, "The First Declaration of Human Rights," http://www.vohuman.org/Articles/The%20First%20 Declaration%20of%20Human%20Rights.htm.

[2] Jack Donnelly, *Universal Human Rights in Theory and Practice* (Ithaca, N.Y.: Cornell University Press, 1989), 60.

[3] For a more extensive discussion of these points, see Burns H. Weston, "Human Rights," *New Encyclopedia Britannica*, 15th ed., vol. 20 (Chicago: Encyclopedia Britannica, Inc., 2002), 657–658.

[4] See Ronald Dworkin, *Taking Rights Seriously* (Cambridge, Mass.: Harvard University Press, 1977), xi.

[5] An excellent analysis of the meaning of the UDHR is in Mary Ann Glendon, "Knowing the Universal Declaration," *Notre Dame Law Review* 73 (1998): 1153–1182.

[6] Weston, "Human Rights," 658.

[7] See, for example, Mary Ann Glendon, *A World Made New: Eleanor Roosevelt and the Universal Declaration of Human Rights* (New York: Random House, 2001); Mary Ann Glendon, "Foundations of Human Rights," *American Journal of Jurisprudence* 44 (1999): 1–14; Susan Waltz, "Universalizing Human Rights: The Role of Small States in the Construction of the Universal Declaration of Human Rights," *Human Rights Quarterly* 23 (2001): 44–72; Susan Waltz, "Universal Human Rights: The Contribution of Muslim States," *Human Rights Quarterly*, 26 (2004): 799–844.

[8] Glendon, "Foundations of Human Rights," 6.

[9] Waltz, "Universal Human Rights: The Contribution of Muslim States."

[10] See Richard Falk, "A Half Century of Human Rights: Geopolitics and Values," in *The Future of International Human Rights*, ed. Burns H. Weston and Stephen P. Marks (Ardsley, N.Y.: Transnational Publishers, 1999), 2–3.

[11] On the historical development of human rights ideas both leading up to the UDHR and afterward, see Paul Gordon Lauren, *The Evolution of International Human Rights: Visions Seen* (Philadelphia: University of Pennsylvania, 1998). See also Carla Hesse and Robert Post, eds., *Human Rights in Political Transitions: Gettysburg to Bosnia* (Cambridge, Mass.: MIT Press, 1999).

[12] See, for example, Amnesty International-Library-Human rights and sexual orientation and gender identity AI INDEX: ACT 79/001/2004, March 31, 2004, http://web.amnesty.org/library/print/ENGACT790012004; Amnesty International-Library-UN Commission on Human Rights: Universality under threat over sexual orientation resolution AI INDEX: IOR 41/013/2003, April 22, 2003, Amnesty International Press Release, http://web.amnesty.org/library/print/ENGIOR410132003. On protections for homosexuals that have recently developed in the European system, see Travis J. Langenkamp, "Finding Fundamental Fairness: Protecting the Rights of Homosexuals Under European Union Accession Law," *San Diego International Law Journal* 4 (2003): 437–465.

[13] For a critical dissection of the treatment of rights in the Cairo Declaration, see Ann Elizabeth Mayer, *Islam and Human Rights: Tradition and Politics,* 3rd ed. (Boulder, Colo.: Westview, 1999) 80, 86–87, 89, 96, 120–121, 146–147, 172, 204, 206–208. For a favorable evaluation of the Cairo Declaration and other efforts to craft distinctive Islamic human rights standards to govern Muslims, see generally Mashood A. Baderin, *International Human Rights and Islamic Law* (Oxford: Oxford University Press, 2004).

[14] See generally Ann Elizabeth Mayer, "Universal versus Islamic Human Rights: A Clash of Cultures or a Clash with a Construct?" *Michigan Journal of International Law* 15 (1994): 307–404.

[15] See, for example, Ann Elizabeth Mayer, "Shifting Grounds for Challenging the Authority of International Human Rights Law: Religion as a Malleable and Politicized Pretext for Governmental Noncompliance with Human Rights," in *Human Rights with Modesty: The Problem of Universalism,* ed. Andras Sajo (Leiden: Martinus Nijhoff, 2004), 349–374. I have argued that "Islamic" reservations about the Women's Convention deserve critical examination; see Ann Elizabeth Mayer, "Religious Reservations to the Convention on the Elimination of All Forms of Discrimination Against Women: What Do They Really Mean?" in *Religious Fundamentalisms and the Human Rights of Women,* ed. Courtney Howland (New York: St. Martin's Press, 1999), 105–127, and "Internationalization of the Conversation on Women's Rights: Arab Governments Face the CEDAW Committee" in *Islamic Law and the Challenge of Modernity,* ed. Yvonne Haddad and Barbara Freyer Stowasser (New York: Altamira Press, 2004), 133–160.

[16] For a comparison of international human rights law and rights provisions in the U.S. Constitution, see Joseph Wronka, *Human Rights and Social Policy in the 21st Century* (Lanham, Md.: University Press of America, 1998), 135–157.

[17] See Gertrude Himmelfarb, *The Roads to Modernity* (New York: Knopf, 2004).

[18] The rationale for disregarding second-generation rights has occasionally been challenged. See, for example, Cass R. Sunstein, *The Second Bill of Rights: FDR's Unfinished Revolution and Why We Need It More Than Ever* (New York: Basic Books, 2004).

[19] See Richard A. Primus, *The American Language of Rights* (New York: Cambridge University Press, 1999).

[20] For a discussion of the intensifying controversies about the way U.S. law lags behind international law, see the articles collected in "Agora: The United

States Constitution and International Law," *American Journal of International Law* 98 (2004): 42–108.

[21] See the Constitutional Preservation Resolution at http://thomas.loc .gov/cgi-bin/query/z?c108:H.+Res.+446:

[22] See "United Nations: World Conference on Human Rights, Vienna Declaration and Programme of Action," New York 1993, A/CONF.157/23, July 12, 1993, par. 18, http://www.unhchr.ch/huridocda/huridoca.nsf/(Symbol)/A .CONF.157.23.En?OpenDocument.

[23] Information on the U.S. Office of International Religious Freedom, which monitors religious persecution and discrimination and recommends policies, can be found at http://www.state.gov/g/drl/irf/.

[24] See International Religious Freedom Report, released by the Bureau of Democracy, Human Rights and Labor, 2003, Executive Summary, http:// www.state.gov/g/drl/rls/irf/2003/27185.htm.

[25] Details of the different patterns of religious discrimination can be found in *U.S. State Department Country Reports on Human Rights Practices* and in the *International Religious Freedom Report for 2003,* http://www.state.gov/g/ drl/rls/irf/2003/.

[26] The impact of the experience of European imperialism and how it shapes Muslims' reactions to U.S. intervention in the Middle East is discussed in a recent work by Rashid Khalidi. See Rashid Khalidi, *Western Footprints and America's Perilous Path in the Middle East* (Boston: Beacon Press, 2004).

[27] Of course, concerns for Muslims' thwarted liberation struggles in other places like Chechnya and Kashmir also play a role in Muslims' elevating self-determination to the status of a particularly central human right.

[28] Council of the League of Arab States, Arab Charter on Human Rights, September 15, 1994, reprinted in *Human Rights Law Journal* 18 (1997): 151; available at http://www1.umn.edu/humanrts/instree/arabcharter.html.

[29] The Casablanca Declaration of the Arab Human Rights Movement, adopted by the First International Conference of the Arab Human Rights Movement, Casablanca, April 23–25, 1999, available at http://www.al-bab.com/arab/docs/international/hr1999.htm.

[30] See the discussion in Ann Elizabeth Mayer, "War and Peace in the Islamic Tradition and International Law," in *Just War and Jihad: Historical and Theoretical Perspectives on War and Peace in Western and Islamic Traditions,* ed. James Turner Johnson and John Kelsay (Westport, Conn.: Greenwood Press, 1991), 209–217.

[31] The Cairo Declaration of Human Rights in Islam, 19th Islamic Conference of Foreign Ministers, Cairo, August 5, 1990, available at http://www.mfa.gov.eg/getdoc.asp?id=134&cat=030305.

[32] "Doha Declaration for Democracy and Reform," *The Daily Star* (Beirut), June 29, 2004, available at http://www.dailystar.com.lb/article.asp?edition_id=10&categ_id=15&article_id=5705#.

[33] Casablanca Declaration.

[34] See Jim Lobe, "Losing Arab Hearts and Minds—It's the Policy, Stupid. Analysis," *InterPressService*, July 23, 2004, http://www.ipsnews.net/interna.asp?idnews=24768.

[35] See Khalidi, *Resurrecting Empire*.

[36] See, for example, Roger Cohen, "Strange Bedfellows: 'Imperial America' Retreats from Iraq," *New York Times*, July 4, 2004, sec. 4, 6.

[37] See William Wallis, "Arab fears of another western intervention as Sudan crisis deepens," *Financial Times*, August 3, 2004, 7.

[38] Colum Lynch, "Islamic Bloc, Christian Right Team Up to Lobby U.N.," *Washington Post*, June 17, 2002, A10.

[39] Ibid.

CHAPTER THREE

A DISTINCTLY ISLAMIC VIEW OF HUMAN RIGHTS
DOES IT EXIST AND IS IT COMPATIBLE WITH THE UNIVERSAL DECLARATION OF HUMAN RIGHTS?

Khaled Abou El Fadl

In answer to the question, "Is there a distinctly Islamic view of human rights, and if so, is it compatible with the Universal Declaration of Human Rights?" one must begin by making some important distinctions related to identifying something one can refer to as "belonging to Islam" or to the Islamic tradition. When one talks about the human rights tradition in the West, one can identify the Catholic and Protestant progression in discourses on natural law, and the clear differences between the two approaches, which can be collectively referred to as Christian tradition. When one looks at the Islamic tradition, the situation is more complex.

The reason for this complexity is that some distinctions go beyond the issue of what is Islamic. For example, one important distinction is that between the concept of human rights, on the one hand, and, on the other, international human rights law that emerges from the processes, procedures, and dynamics of the collective system of the United Nations.

DEFINING THE CONCEPT OF HUMAN RIGHTS

The United Nations has its specific mechanisms and processes, which have their own linguistic practice, normative practice, and criteria and system of reference. More importantly, when it comes to making commitments to human rights, the commitment is in the sense of *positive law*; in other words, a commitment is made through an agreement by nations—nations signing a convention or a treaty that binds them in a positive-law fashion to implement certain rules of conduct. The concept of human rights, however, is larger than the process that takes place in the United Nations. It is larger than the Universal Declaration of Human Rights (UDHR) and other positive-law conventions and commitments that ensue from them.

Human rights is fundamentally a rather elusive, perhaps ill-defined, but nevertheless overriding normative concept, very much like the idea of *natural law,* or the idea of the inalienable and inherent. In the other words, human rights is a fundamental moral commitment.

In positive law, what creates the law is the agreement among groups of human beings as reached through parliaments, international institutions, or other forums. These agreements create the law and embody it in various forms of legislation, including international treaties. In sum, within positive law, or a procedural context, a group of people dictate that X is the law.

But what is inalienable and inherent is something that is *above* what people can or cannot agree to. It is, in other words, a right as a matter of right and not of legislation. Therefore, for instance, when it is said, "People have the right to be free," the question arises as to where that right comes from. The answer is that it comes from the very fact that people are human beings and that it is wrong for a human being to be enslaved by another. This means that no political process can ever justify slavery—that no majority, regardless of how large it is, can legislate that slavery is acceptable. In this sense, because human rights as a concept is larger than any process or procedure, it is a normative moral commitment. It is like an ideology. It is self-referential. Its justification is, "It is because it is." And in that sense, it is very much like religion, like belief in God. It is like saying, "I believe in God, not because 100 people agree that God exists, but because I know that God exists. I am sure of it. And if the whole population tells me, or the whole of Congress votes by a 100 percent majority that God does not exist, that is irrelevant to me." Belief in human rights is of a similar nature.

Yet, because human rights is similar to religion in that way, it is possible for people to write a treaty to commit themselves to respect human rights but, because they do not really believe in human rights morally, to end up violating human rights all the time. This also means that it is possible that a nation may not sign any treaty to respect human rights, but may nevertheless respect them because it morally believes in them.

In short, when speaking about human rights, it would be a mistake to think that it is sufficient to discuss what takes place in the United Nations or that by discussing that aspect one has exhausted the topic of human rights. The topic of human rights is much larger philosophically than the legalities and the processes that take place within the administrative and political structure of the UN.

IDENTIFYING A DISTINCTLY ISLAMIC VIEW OF HUMAN RIGHTS

When it comes then to identifying something that one can characterize as distinctly Islamic in regard to human rights, one must take into account that when Muslims engage in the international process involving human rights, other issues are also involved. These issues include concerns about world power and jostling for position, the post–Cold War issues of competition, and the post–Cold War drive for hegemonic dominance. In short, what is taking place is very much part of nationalistic politics, which in many ways is thoroughly secular and is often determined by factors of realpolitik and national interests rather than by an interest in defining what is "real Islam." Therefore, in trying to identify principles and traditions that can be characterized as distinctly Islamic, it is important to account for the political factors and power-related concerns that affect the behavior of Muslim countries.

Consequently, human rights-related documents produced by Arab governments such as the Cairo Declaration (1990), the Arab Charter (1994), the Casablanca Declaration (1999), and the Doha Declaration (2001) are motivated by a desire to engage the international political process far more than to define what is distinctively Islamic. Indeed, many of the provisions of those documents can be interpreted more in terms of the issues of realpolitik and involvement in a nationalistic global context than in terms of concern over defining an Islamic tradition of human rights.

Even the fact that when Muslim nations sign conventions and treaties they condition their commitment, saying that they are bound by those treaties only to the extent that Islamic law permits them, makes no useful contribution in terms of elucidating a distinctly Islamic view of human rights. This is because the conditions are imposed out of concern for issues of realpolitik, power, dominance, and hegemony, and to control the ability of others in determining the fate of Muslim states.

Therefore, before determining whether there is a distinctively Islamic approach to the fundamental notion of human rights, one has to define the concept of human rights. On whatever basis human rights is defined—natural rights, or what is natural to human beings, or conceptions of the well-being of human beings, their dignity, or protection of their rationality—it involves a clear wrestling with the idea of what is necessary by natural reason to protect and preserve a human being.

THE NOTION OF THE SANCTITY OF HUMAN LIFE

On this basis, the answer to whether there is an Islamic response to the above-noted questions or whether there is a distinctively Islamic approach to the fundamental notion of the human being would be, "Yes, but not really." Fundamentally, all conceptions of human rights, as Michael Perry has written, come back to the notion of the sanctity of human life.[1] And it is this sanctity that poses the most imperative question, namely, what is necessary to preserve that life? From this it follows that it is necessary to pay attention to the demands made by human beings. These demands, in turn, create duties toward human beings, which become recognized as rights. This is the philosophical process that takes place—the realization of the sanctity of human life, followed by the realization that the demands made pursuant to the sanctity are necessary, and that those demands give rise to duties, and those duties become the basis for a notion of a fundamental right.

In Islam, clearly there is the idea of the sanctity of human life: there is no question that human life is sanctified. And, indeed, at least in the interpretive communities, by which I mean the communities that interpreted and discoursed about Islam in a textual context—that is, the context of producing texts and producing a common normative language and a common system of symbolisms for discourse about what is Islamic versus what is not Islamic—there is a recognition of the sanctity of human life. There is also a recognition that the sanctity of human life creates demands that, in turn, create duties, which become compelling rights.

TEXTUAL VERSUS CONTEXTUAL INTERPRETATIONS

It may be useful at this point to consider the issue of textual versus contextual interpretations in the Islamic context. The main texts in Islam are the Qur'an and the Sunnah. The Qur'an is considered to be the revealed word of God. The Sunnah, however, was seen as a text but one without a context. In other words, most people believed that there was no creative process in formulating what counts as the Sunnah. I, however, believe that there was a creative process in forming what was to count as textually authoritative in Islam. The text of the Sunnah was developed through a creative process. This means that what was to be included and counted as part of the Sunnah, and what was to be excluded, was a matter of conscious choice. For example, it is well known that Ahmad Ibn Hanbal, after the Inquisition (*Mihna*) that occurred during the ascendancy of the Mu'tazili school under the reign of the Abbasid caliph Mamoun (813–833 CE), refused to narrate or accept any *hadith* (traditions relating to the Prophet's personal actions and words) by an individual who believed that the Qur'an was created, as opposed to uncreated.[2] This was a subjective creative act. When one looks at the text of Ahmad Ibn Hanbal today, it looks objective and canonical. Yet behind those positions was a man who chose what was to be part of the Sunnah.

Even more, the reports that Muslims remembered, of what they said the Prophet said would not be written down for a couple of centuries.[3] So, how does one remember what another human had said? One remembers creatively. In other words, there is a creative process subject to context and, in fact, a cumulative process that goes into *creating* the authoritative hadith. Then there is a creative process subject to context that goes into *recording* the hadith. That is the creativity of the text.

Often one finds traditions in the text that are not a single story, or a single narrative from the beginning to the end. Rather, one often finds competing narratives that mirror different contexts at different times. Thus one finds reports that say, "Dogs and women void prayer;" while another report says, "No, it's not dogs and women; it's women and Jews;" and yet another report says, "No, it was not dogs or women or Jews; the prayer is not voided at all." All of these reports reflect different contexts that are shaping the text—the text of the Sunnah.

Regarding the sanctity of life, there were creative communities that created texts that embodied the concepts of the sanctity of life. Why? First, it was easy to do so because the Qur'an says, "Whoever kills a person, it is as if he kills humanity," and because the Qur'an keeps repeating, "Do not kill, and whoever kills a person, it is as if he kills humanity." Therefore, a considerable amount of the Sunnah affirmed the sanctity of life. However, context, and issues like war and gender, made the application of the concept of sanctity of life complicated. For instance, one began hearing arguments such as, "Well, if you kill a non-Muslim who comes from lands that do not have a treaty with your nation, then you do not get punished for it"; or "The blood money of a woman is half of the blood money of a man"; or "The blood money of a non-Muslim is half of the blood money of a Muslim." So, although the concept of the sanctity of life is still there, the context is modifying it, playing with it and creating layered text—making the text "bumpy" and full of wrinkles. Yet what is striking is how often, despite the intrusion of the context, these interpretive communities of Islam affirm the sanctity of life.

For example, when it comes to an apostate, the interpretive community in Islam would say, "Yes, the text says 'Kill him,' but you cannot do that unless you give him three days and three nights and an opportunity to say the *shahada* ('There is no god but God, and Muhammad is His Prophet'). If he says it, you cannot inquire any further, and you must let him go." Or the interpretive community might talk about such issues as what happens to someone who is a heretic and is spreading poisonous ideas. Do we still respect the sanctity of life? What happens when the Crusaders come and massacre 7,000 Muslims in Antioch? Do we feel the same way about the sanctity of life and still want to affirm it? In other words, the interpretive communities affirmed the sanctity of life in a variety of situations, but because they were human, there was give and take. Because they were human, one does not find them affirming the sanctity of life in an absolute, unwavering, consistent way where no one would ever break the rules.

The process was complicated. Yet it is important to recognize that, throughout this complex interplay, the sanctity of life remains a constant theme. Normatively we now have our own context, and our own context might allow us to preserve the sanctity of life more than previous contexts did.

Therefore, if we keep in mind that the text was creatively formed, giving expression to a variety of contexts, then we do not expect from the text what we are not going to find. In other words, we do not deal with the text ahistorically and ask questions like, "Why doesn't the text defend the right to this, and the right to that?", and so on. We understand that the text is really a tapestry that reflects various contexts and orientations. When I open up books on *Shari'a*, they all have different contexts and different timeframes and show people struggling with the essential issue of the sanctity of life. Now I am struggling with it in the same way earlier thinkers and scholars did, and I have a context of my own. And I cannot deny that I am going to try to preserve the sanctity of life according to my context—and there is nothing wrong with that. In fact, that is not only legitimate, but also expected.

That is part of the sociology of human existence—that all of us achieve things within the limits of how far our consciousness and our hearts and minds have been able to absorb a particular time and a place. Within my context, I am going to try to preserve the sanctity of life.

We are not at a point, for instance, for me to say that we should reject the use of violence in all situations, as Gandhi did, because in our context there need to be wars of self-defense; people need the ability to go to war when they are attacked. Our context does not allow me to become a Gandhian. But maybe someday we can all become Gandhians. And so comes the same idea, namely, where the Qur'an sets the moral objective—the moral trajectory—and we try to realize it as much as we can within our particular contexts. It is moronic to judge the people of a different context and a different time and ask, "Why did not they achieve what I achieve now?"

PROTECTING THE SANCTITY OF HUMAN LIFE

Is there a distinctively Islamic response to the question of what is necessary by natural reason to protect and preserve a human being?

Interestingly, it is exactly this type of question that produced the most intriguing concept in Islamic tradition—*huquq Allah*, literally "the rights of God," versus *huquq al-'ibad*, "the rights of people" —and produced within Islamic discourse the most intriguing statements, namely that the fulfillment of the rights of people takes priority over fulfillment of the rights of God. It is quite remarkable that such a position developed in the twelfth century.

Let us not forget that when Thomas Aquinas was wrestling with issues of human dignity in the following century and said that the first principle of human law is to call for the good and forbid what is bad, that concept already existed in Islam in the injunction *al-amr bi'l ma'ruf wa al-nahy 'ann al-munkar* (enjoining the good and forbidding the evil). Indeed, it is possible and even likely that, because he was quite aware of several important aspects of the Islamic tradition, Aquinas was influenced by that tradition in deducting his first principle of natural law.

Here we are fundamentally talking about where it is possible for the human rights tradition and Islam to meet. Muslim jurists[4] began by contemplating the laws that God decreed. They observed that some of these laws seem to protect things that belong to God, like the law of prayer or the law of fasting. Other laws seem to protect the rights of human beings —laws like "Thou shalt not kill," "You cannot steal," "You cannot cheat," "If you enter into a contract, bring witnesses," "Before you convict someone of a crime, presume them innocent," or "Before you convict someone of a crime, you have to bring witnesses."

The Muslim jurists recognized that these laws did not protect God or the rights of God, but rather, they protected the rights of human beings. The jurists then went further, saying that in the universe God has certain things that God protects, and certain things that God has said human beings ought to protect. The Muslim jurists said that God is protecting His rights through the laws that He set down. But there is evidence that God recognizes that human beings have their own set of rights, and that those rights must be protected for the sake of human beings, not for the sake of God.

The jurists also said that as far as the rights of God are concerned, only God has a possessory power over those rights. By contrast, in regard to the rights of human beings, it is the human beings who have the possessory power.

So God protects His own rights and human beings protect their own rights. Now, what if in terms of guarding and protecting these rights, God protects His rights in the Hereafter. In other words, in the Hereafter God will punish those who did not pray and those who did not fast. But what do human beings do? Human beings take care of the rights of other human beings on this earth.

So what are these rights? Muslim jurists of all schools of jurisprudence recognized the following rights for people:

1. the right to life;

2. the right to property;

3. the right to one's reputation (i.e., being free from slander);

4. the right to lineage (i.e., marriage, having children, and protecting the name of the family); and

5. the right to intellect (i.e., the right to stay sober, to develop one's intellect, to read and learn, and to believe in whatever one wants to believe).

The jurists argued that a government should concern itself with protecting these rights.[5] How, for example, does one deal with the issue of the clash between the rights of God and the rights of people? The best example of this may be in the case of theft. If someone steals from someone else, he or she has also stolen something that is that person's right, namely the right to property. Muslim jurists argued that neither the state nor God can have the power to forgive the taking of a person's property. Only the person who was robbed has the power to forgive, because only that person is the possessor of the right. Therefore the state is obligated to bring back property that was stolen from a person. The state cannot say, "We forgive it, it is okay." Likewise, on the Final Day God will not forgive the stealing of a person's property unless the person who was wronged forgives the stealing of his or her property. God's forgiveness is dependent on the wronged person's forgiveness because it involves a human right.

Similarly, if someone slanders another, the state cannot say, "We do not care about the slander." If someone takes away, hurts, or damages another's reputation, God will not forgive that on the Final Day unless the wronged person forgives it, or unless the person who has done the wrong comes and begs forgiveness from the injured person, or accepts punishment for it. With punishment, it is as if the right of the wronged person has been restored. In Islamic law, the person who has been wronged has the right to demand compensation, or to demand punishment, or to forgive.

THE ORIGIN OF RIGHTS: TWO VIEWS

What is the basis for human beings having these rights? Where did these rights come from? God's rights came from God declaring, "These are My rights." But where did the rights of humans come from? Here there were two very distinct views.

One school maintained that human rights come from God—that God said, "These are the rights of human beings." Another school held, "No, it is not that God said these are the rights of human beings. Rather, it is the very act of creation that gives human beings these rights." The holders of this view argued that, human beings became endowed with these rights immediately upon their creation. Theoretically, then, if human beings were created by someone other than God, they would still have the same rights, such as the presumption of innocence; this school argued, "Do we need a law that says everyone is presumed to be innocent unless proven otherwise? Or do we assume by philosophical positioning that everyone is innocent unless proven otherwise?"

The adherents of this school believed that the issue of rights was like the nature of a falsity or truth. As one jurist belonging to this school said, "If I was walking and I heard a voice from the sky saying, 'I am God and it is okay to lie,' I would not lie. It would still be wrong to lie." The other school maintained that God gave human beings these rights and that God could have given human beings other rights than these or could have not recognized these rights. This is a very important distinction between the two schools. According to the first school, these rights become inherent and inalienable, and the only question then becomes how does one protect them.

POSITIVE LAW VERSUS THE RIGHTS OF THE PEOPLE

By the sixth Islamic century (twelfth century CE), the concepts of *huquq Allah* (the rights of God), and *huquq al-'ibad* (the rights of people) were recognized—even to the point that the rights of people were given priority over the rights of God—and the idea that it is a duty to enjoin the good and forbid the evil was developed. However, an important question remained concerning these rights, namely, is it positive law that defines the rights of the people, or do the rights of the people define the law? In other words, there exists the conception of sanctity of human life, the conception of demands and reciprocal obligations or duties, and the resulting conception of the rights of people. The remaining question is what happens if these conceptions clash with the positive law as deduced from the text—as read and interpreted from the text. Do the rights take priority over the text, or does the text take priority over the rights?

For example, people have a right to intellect. If the text says that an apostate should be killed, however, this clashes with the philosophical awareness that people have a right to their intellect, which seems to mean that people have a right not to believe. So which one wins? Does the right win or does the text win?

Some jurists, such as those belonging to the Mu'tazili school, took the position that the very existence of such a clash meant either the text is not authentic or that it has not been interpreted correctly, because the text should never clash with a right that belongs to a human being. Other jurists, such as those belonging to the school of Ahl al-Hadith, disagreed. They argued that once the text says something, it is as if God has given those rights to human beings, so God can limit the extent to which humans can exercise their rights.

So there is consistency in these competing positions. Those who believed that God gave rights to human beings also believed that God can set limits—that God can punish apostasy, for instance, or that God can forbid the reading of heretical books. In contrast, those who thought that these rights are inherent and fundamental believed that the text can never take away these rights. Therefore, the law of apostasy must be wrong because it clashes with the right of intellect, or a law banning one from reading or learning whatever one wants must be wrong because it clashes with a fundamental right.

The former view is consistent with the Wahhabi view today. The Wahhabis do not recognize any inherent fundamental rights. Rather, they believe that all rights come from the text—that the text defines the rights a human being has and that the text takes away the rights a human being has. Inconsistently, however, they also think that public interest, which is not based on a text, can take away a right even if given by a text.

Thomas Aquinas turned the concept of enjoining the good and forbidding the evil into an active, dynamic, and evolving concept that was able to strike down various laws that obstructed the conception of the good and the conception of the evil. He argued that there is a first principle of good and bad—the first principle in nature—that one must do good and forbid evil. And he built an entire philosophical edifice based on the premise that one must command the good and forbid the evil, which begged the question "What is good and what is evil?"

From there, Thomas Aquinas went on to define good and evil. The basis of all natural law, according to him, is that one must command the good and forbid the evil. As noted earlier, Islam has the same principle (*al-amr bi'l ma'ruf wa al-nahy 'ann al-munkar*). Indeed, I think that Thomas Aquinas based his whole theory of natural law on this principle. Unfortunately, Muslims did not do as much with that very important principle.

By the fourth Islamic century (tenth century CE), there was a growing reluctance among Muslim jurists to allow the conception of the sanctity of human life to strike down positive law (i.e., interpretations of the text), and by the twelfth century there were practically no voices that allowed the normative commitment to the sanctity of human life to have a sort of veto power over positive law. Increasingly, the Islamic era saw a greater reliance on positive law and less reliance on inherent rights or a philosophy of rights. For instance, during the earlier days of Islam, one could say that slavery is inconsistent with the protection of human rights. Umar ibn al-Khattab (the second caliph) said that people were born free and how could you enslave them? And he could build a whole set of laws on that principle. But as time went by, Muslims became far more reluctant to recognize such general principles and to deduce laws from them. Rather, they increasingly respected the positive law at the expense of general moral principles such as people are born free.

What produced this dynamic? As Islamic civilization became exposed to more and more dangers and clashed with more enemies, it became increasingly conservative.

RECONCILING CONCEPTIONS OF HUMAN RIGHTS

Conservatism had existed from the fourth century (tenth century CE) onward in Islam, but the level of conservatism had fluctuated. There were conservative periods and there were liberal periods. In liberal periods, there was an openness toward philosophy and notions of inherent rights, and in conservative periods, there was a conservatism that rejected these types of moral generalities

Over time, however, a theoretical impasse developed. And to this very day, people who have tried to work with Islamic conceptions of human rights, including modern scholars, have not addressed this fundamental question. Rather, they basically have said that there is no contradiction between the Islamic tradition and notions of human rights, because in Islam there is the concept of *maslahah*, (public good), or because in Islam *ijtihad* (exercising one's independent judgment) is possible.

In other words, modern scholars have been looking for a sort of comforting symbolic language that says we have, in the Islamic discourse, ideas that can solve the problem of the compatibility of Islamic tradition with notions of human rights. But the fundamental problem remains; namely, can whatever is rationally deduced as necessary to maintain the sanctity of human life prevail and have a prior order over the textually deduced law? Or is the opposite true, namely, that the textually deduced law basically trumps any conception of sanctity of life, and therefore one must simply stop with textual interpretation and not consider the notions of inherent rights?

That is a fundamental issue, and there is an extreme reluctance among modern scholars to recognize it or to deal with it. In fact, in my own sometimes-interesting experience, the attempt to deal with this question has quickly brought about accusations of being *zindiq* (heretic), or *mu'tazili*, or "secret Shi'i," and other forms of deviation from mainstream Islam.

Everyone who talks about Islamic law and human rights refers first to the positive law. The positive law says, "Kill the apostate." The positive law does not believe in the rights of women or in protecting the rights of children, and so forth. Instead of saying, "There is a moral principle that overrides these positive laws, and we must rethink these positive laws and creatively generate new positive laws that affirm the moral principle," people say, "There is no incompatibility between Islamic law and human rights because we have maslahah, or we have ijtihad, and we can use these to reconcile any conflicts." When it comes to talking about specific laws, however, and whether they are valid, nothing is done. Take, for example, the law that a husband cannot go to prison for striking his wife, or the law that a woman inherits only half of what a man inherits, or that the testimony of a woman counts as only half of the testimony of a man in certain circumstances, or that it is possible to execute someone who insults the Prophet. Do these modern scholars use maslahah or ijtihad to uphold the principle of human rights? They do not—because they do not have a clear view or a clear understanding of the normative moral commitment that Islam makes. For example, a large number of people think that the law that a woman inherits half of what a man inherits in many situations is the normative commitment itself. They believe that that is the moral commitment and that therefore one must protect that law regardless of the circumstances. I am saying, "No, that is the positive law; that is not a moral commitment." And herein lies the difference.

We must distinguish between what in the text is a moral commitment—to establish justice, for instance, or to establish mercy—and what in the text is a positive law. Ijtihad and maslahah are simply mechanisms. People feel good knowing that they have the mechanisms, but they lack the courage to use them. Merely stating that Islam has the concepts of maslahah and ijtihad is not enough to clarify or elucidate the moral commitments. One does not start with the tools. One must start with Islam's moral commitments.

HARVESTING THE SEEDS OF AN ISLAMIC VIEW OF HUMAN RIGHTS

Until this issue is dealt with and treated theologically and philosophically, the answer to whether there is a distinctly Islamic view of human rights must be that there are only the seeds of an Islamic view of human rights.

In this context, there once was considerable thinking about the normative commitments of Islam—what are the moral commitments of Islam? what are the basic ethics of Islam? The people who created the theory about the rights of God and the rights of people and mixed rights were part of this process of creative thinking. For a long time now, however, people have stopped thinking about those issues. Instead, they have become obsessed with positive law. Those who did the original thinking left behind seeds of ideas. But those grand ideas did not develop into major intellectual traditions. Unlike the natural law tradition, which began with the idea of enjoining the good and forbidding the evil and evolved into this huge edifice of theory upon theory of natural law—such as whether natural law is intuitively realized, or is rationally realized, and so forth—the concepts of the moral commitments and basic ethics of Islam did not go any further.

So what is needed now? Muslims need someone to go back and to think of things like the rights of God versus the rights of people. They have to question what the moral commitments of Islam are. What is it that Islam wants to do with humanity?

Muslims for the most part do not ask questions like that anymore. They read the Qur'anic verse in which God tells the Prophet, "You were sent as a mercy to humankind." This is a seed. But no one thinks about the full implications of the Prophet being a mercy to humankind. Muslims must sit down and think out all of the philosophical implications of that verse. That is how they can nurture and harvest a seed.

In sum, the answer to the question of whether there is "a distinctly Islamic view of human rights" and whether that view is compatible with the Universal Declaration of Human Rights is that there are seeds in Islamic tradition that have been lying about on the ground since the twelfth century, waiting to be brought to life—seeds that could give rise to an Islamic view of human rights compatible with the UDHR. To develop these seeds into a comprehensive Islamic view of human rights is the principal challenge facing Muslims today, especially Muslim thinkers, scholars, and religious leaders.

Notes

[1] Michael J. Perry, *The Idea of Human Rights: Four Inquiries* (Oxford: Oxford University Press, 1998).

[2] The fundamental debate between the Hanbalis and the Mu'tazili related to the issue of whether the Qur'an was created or uncreated. Those like Ibn Hanbal who believed in the uncreatedness of the Qur'an maintained that it existed primordially; in other words, it coexisted with God. The Mu'tazili believed that it was created by God. For a discussion of these issues, see Richard C. Martins and Mark R. Woodward with Dwi S. Atmaja, *Defenders of Reason in Islam: Mutazilism from Medieval School to Modern Symbol* (Oxford: Oneworld Publications, 1997).

[3] When exactly the written documentation of hadith occurred is a matter of considerable scholarly debate. Some believe it commenced immediately

after the death of the Prophet. Others believe it did not commence until 100 to 200 years after the death of the Prophet. See Khaled Abou El Fadl, *Speaking In God's Name* (Oxford: Oneworld Publications, 2001).

[4] It is not clear which school was the first to develop the concept of the rights of God versus the rights of people; however, this concept was eventually adopted by all Islamic schools of jurisprudence.

[5] Some jurists such as Abd al Rahman ibn Amr al Awza'i debated whether there are five rights or more. See Marwan Muhammad Sha'ar, *al-Awza'i, imam al-salaf* (Beirut: Dar al Nafa'is, 1992).

CHAPTER FOUR

WOMEN'S RIGHTS IN ISLAM
NORMATIVE TEACHINGS VERSUS PRACTICE

Riffat Hassan

The subject of this chapter is women's rights in Islam. Its main purpose is to identify the rights given to women by the Qur'an and to point out the discrepancy between the normative teachings of Islam and Muslim practice regarding issues dealing with women's status and rights. However, the subject of "women in Islam" cannot be properly understood if looked at in isolation from the important issues facing Muslim societies—issues that do not reflect either Islam or the Islamic tradition.

In view of the intense interest in the West regarding the rights and status of Muslim women, this subject should also be examined in the context of the overall relations between the West and the Islamic world.

WESTERN IMAGES OF ISLAM AND MUSLIMS

Since the 1970s there has been a growing interest in the West regarding Islam and Muslims, an interest further intensified after the tragic events of 9/11. However, much of this interest has been limited to a few subjects, such as "the Islamic revival," "Islamic fundamentalism," "the Salman Rushdie affair," "women in Islam," and, since 9/11, Islamic terrorism. It has not involved an effort to understand either the complexity or the diversity of "the World of Islam." Moreover, the subjects chosen have tended to evoke or provoke strong emotive responses among both Westerners and Muslims. Also, the manner in which these subjects have generally been portrayed in the Western media or popular literature has called into question the motivation underlying the selective Western interest in Islam and Muslims. As a result, many

Muslims have found it difficult to see this interest as being positively motivated.

These negative images and interpretations of Islam in the West exert a strong influence because they are rooted in much older Western perceptions of Islam as reflected in the views of two major Western literary and religious figures. Dante, the great poet of medieval Christianity, perceived the Prophet of Islam as the "divider of the world of Christendom" and assigned him to the lowest level of hell for his grievous "sin." St. Thomas Aquinas, the outstanding scholastic philosopher who owed such a profound debt to the thinkers of Muslim Spain, described Islam as nothing but a construct to accommodate the lust of Muhammad.[1] What far-reaching shadows were cast upon the future by powerful Christian voices such as those of Dante and Aquinas can be glimpsed from Thomas Carlyle's historic lecture on "The Hero as Prophet—Mahomet: Islam" in the series entitled *On Heroes, Hero-Worship and The Heroic in History*. Writing in the mid-nineteenth-century, Carlyle urged his fellow Christians to dismiss *"our current hypothesis* about Mahomet, that he was a scheming Imposter, a Falsehood Incarnate, that his religion is a mere quackery and fatuity."[2]

Given the historical and more recent reservoir of negative images associated with Islam and Muslims in the West, the outpouring of so much sympathy in and by the West toward Muslim women appears, at least to Muslims, to be an amazing contradiction. For are Muslim women also not adherents of Islam? This broader context of Western-Muslim relations should thus be kept in mind in discussing women's rights in Islam, which currently is one of the issues that divides the West and the Muslim world in regard to human rights in general.

MUSLIM WOMEN AND HUMAN RIGHTS: THE UNARTICULATED QUANDARY

Because the modern notion of human rights originated in a Western, secular context, Muslims in general, but Muslim women in particular, find themselves in a quandary when they initiate or participate in a discussion on human rights, whether in the West or in Muslim societies. Based on their life experience, most Muslim women who become human rights advocates or activists feel strongly that virtually all Muslim societies discriminate against women from cradle to grave. This leads many of them to become deeply alienated from Muslim culture in a number of ways, and their strong sense of alienation often leads to anger and bitterness toward the patriarchal systems of thought and social structures that dominate most Muslim societies.

Muslim women often find much support and sympathy in the West so long as they are seen as rebels and deviants within the world of Islam. But many of them begin to realize, sooner or later, that while they have serious difficulties with Muslim culture, they also are not able, for many reasons, to completely identify with Western culture. This realization leads them to feel—at least for a time—isolated and alone. Much attention has been focused in the Western media and literature on the sorry plight of Muslim women who are "poor and oppressed" in visible or tangible ways. Hardly any notice has been taken, however, of the profound tragedy and trauma suffered by the self-aware Muslim women of today who are struggling to maintain their religious identity and personal autonomy in the face of the intransigence of Muslim culture, on the one hand, and the hedgemonistic aspirations of Western culture, on the other.

SOURCES OF THE ISLAMIC TRADITION

Before one can speak meaningfully about women in the context of Islam or the Islamic tradition, it is necessary to clarify what is meant by "the Islamic tradition," which—like other major religious traditions—does not consist of or derive from a single source. Most Muslims, if questioned about its sources, are likely to refer to more than one of the following:

- the Qur'an, or the Book of Revelation that Muslims believe to be God's word transmitted through the agency of the Archangel Gabriel to the Prophet Muhammad;

- *Sunnah*, or the practical traditions of the Prophet Muhammad;

- *hadith*, or the oral sayings attributed to the Prophet Muhammad;

- *fiqh* (jurisprudence) or *madhahib* (schools of law); and

- the *Shari'a*, or code of law that regulates the diverse aspects of a Muslim's life.

Although these sources have contributed to what is cumulatively referred to as the Islamic tradition, they are not identical or considered to be of equal weight. Of all the sources of the Islamic tradition, the most important is the Qur'an, which is regarded by Muslims in general as having absolute authority.

Yet, although the Qur'an has always been, in theory, *the* primary and most authoritative source of normative Islam since the early days of Islam, the hadith literature has been the lens through which the words of the Qur'an have been seen and interpreted. It has been the consensus of hadith scholars from the time of Imam Al-Bukhari (194–265 AH)—considered by Sunni Muslims to be the most highly authoritative scholar of hadith—that the vast majority of *ahadith* are, in fact, not authentic. What the hadith literature contains, in other words, are not so much the words of the Prophet of Islam, but a representation of the Arab-Islamic culture of seventh- and eighth-century Muslims. This culture was influenced significantly by earlier religious and philosophical traditions and incorporated many of the prevalent Jewish, Christian, Hellenistic, pre-Islamic Bedouin, and other negative ideas and attitudes regarding women. These ideas and traditions have been used throughout Muslim history to undermine the intent of the Qur'an to liberate women from the status of chattels or inferior creatures and make them free and equal to men.

Moreover, throughout Islamic history, the sources for the Islamic tradition have been interpreted only by Muslim men, who have arrogated to themselves the task of defining the ontological, theological, sociological, and eschatalogical status of Muslim women. While it is encouraging to know that women such as Khadijah and A'ishah (wives of the Prophet Muhammad) and Rabi'a al-Basri (the outstanding woman Sufi) figure significantly in early Islam, the fact remains that until the present time the Islamic tradition has been largely patriarchal, inhibiting the growth of scholarship among women, particularly in the realm of religious thought.

Given this state of affairs, it is hardly surprising that until recently the vast majority of Muslim women have remained wholly or largely unaware of their "Islamic" (in an ideal sense) rights. Male-centered and male-dominated Muslim societies have continued to assert, glibly and tirelessly, that Islam has given women more rights than any other religion, while keeping women in physical, mental, and emotional confinement and depriving them of the opportunity to actualize their human potential. This is illustrated by the high level of illiteracy among Muslim women, especially those living in rural areas (where most of the Muslim population lives).

THE QUR'AN'S ETHICAL FRAMEWORK AND THE RIGHTS OF MUSLIM WOMEN

The Qur'an's vision of human destiny is embodied in the exalted proclamation, "Towards God is thy limit."[3] To enable men and women to achieve this destiny and discharge the responsibility of being God's vicegerent (*khalifah*) upon the earth, the Qur'an affirms fundamental rights that all human beings ought to have because these rights are so deeply rooted in their humanness that their denial or violation is tantamount to a negation or degradation of that which makes people human. From the perspective of the Qur'an, these rights came into existence when humans did. They were created, as humans were, by God, in order that human potential could be actualized. Not only do they provide human beings with the opportunity to develop all their inner resources; they also uphold before them a vision of what God would like them to strive for. Rights given by God are eternal and immutable and cannot be abolished by any temporal ruler or human agency.

Because the Qur'an is concerned about all human beings and all aspects of life, it contains references to a large number of human rights. Among these rights, the following are particularly noteworthy:

The right to life. The Qur'an upholds the sanctity and absolute value of human life,[4] and points out that, in essence, the life of each individual is comparable to that of an entire community and therefore should be treated with utmost care.[5]

The right to respect. According to the Qur'an, humanity was appointed God's vicegerent on earth because of all creation it alone had the ability to think, to have knowledge of good and evil, to do the right and avoid the wrong. Thus, on account of the promise that is contained in being human, the humanness of all human beings is to be respected.

The right to justice. The Qur'an puts great emphasis on the right to seek justice and the duty to do justice.[6] In the context of justice, the

Qur'an uses two concepts: *adl* and *ihsan*. *Adl* is justice in a legalistic sense and is represented by a scale that is evenly balanced. It is in the spirit of *adl* that special merit must be considered in matters of rewards and that special circumstances are to be considered in matters of punishments. For instance, for crimes of unchastity the Qur'an prescribes identical punishments for a man or a woman who is proved guilty,[7] but it differentiates between different classes of women: for the same crime, a slave woman would receive half, and the Prophet's consort double, the punishment given to a "free" Muslim woman.[8] In making such a distinction, the Qur'an, while upholding high moral standards, particularly in the case of the Prophet's wives (whose actions had a normative significance for the community), reflects God's compassion for women slaves, who were socially disadvantaged.

Ihsan goes beyond *adl* and refers to a restoring of balance by making up a loss or deficiency. To understand this concept, it is necessary to understand the nature of the *ummah* (ideal community) envisaged by the Qur'an. *Ummah* comes from the root *umm,* which means "mother." Thus the ummah is likened to a mother. The symbols of a mother and motherly love and compassion are also linked with the two attributes most characteristic of God, namely *Rahman* (compassionate) and *Rahim,* (merciful), both of which are derived from the root *rahm,* which means "womb." The ideal ummah cares about all its members just as an ideal mother cares about all her children, knowing that all are not equal and that each has different needs. A mother who makes up for the deficiency of a disadvantaged child exemplifies the spirit of *ihsan*. *Ihsan* thus shows God's sympathy for the disadvantaged segments of human society such as women, children, slaves, the poor, and the infirm.

The right to freedom. A large part of the Qur'an's concern is to free human beings from the chains that bind them: traditionalism, authoritarianism (religious, political, economic), tribalism, racism, classism or caste system, sexism, and slavery. The greatest guarantee of personal freedom for a Muslim lies in the Qur'anic decree that no one other than God can limit human freedom,[9] and that judgment regarding what is right or wrong rests with God alone.[10] In political matters, the Qur'an makes the principle of mutual consultation (*shura*) mandatory[11] and gives to responsible dissent the status of a fundamental right.[12] The Qur'anic proclamation that there shall be no coercion in matters of faith[13] guarantees freedom of religion and worship. The right to freedom includes the right to be free to testify to the truth. Standing up for the truth is a right and a responsibility that a Muslim may not disclaim even in the face of the greatest danger or difficulty.[14] At the same time that the Qur'an commands believers to testify to the truth, it also instructs society not to harm persons so testifying.[15]

The right to privacy. The Qur'an recognizes the need for privacy as a human right and lays down rules for protecting an individual's life in the home from undue intrusion from within or without.[16]

The right to protection from slander, backbiting, and ridicule. The Qur'an recognizes the right of human beings to be protected from defamation, sarcasm, offensive nicknames, and backbiting.[17] It also states that no person is to be maligned on grounds of assumed guilt.[18]

The right to acquire knowledge. The Qur'an puts the highest emphasis on the importance of acquiring knowledge, which is regarded as a prerequisite for the creation of a just world in which authentic peace can prevail.

The right to sustenance. A cardinal concept in the Qur'an, one that underlies the socioeconomic-political system of Islam, is that the ownership of everything belongs, not to any person, but to God. Because God is the universal creator, every creature has the right to partake of what belongs to God.[19] This means that every human being has the right to a means to a living and that those who hold economic or political power do not have the right to deprive others of the basic necessities of life by misappropriating or misusing resources that have been created by God for the benefit of humanity in general.

The right to work. According to Qur'anic teaching, every man and woman has the right to work, whether the work consists of gainful employment or voluntary service. The fruits of labor belong to the one who has worked for them, regardless of whether it is a man or a woman.[20]

The right to develop one's aesthetic responsibilities and enjoy the bounties created by God. As pointed out by Muhammad Asad, "By declaring that all good and beautiful things in life, i.e., those that are not expressly prohibited—are lawful to the believers, the Qur'an condemns,

by implication all forms of life-denying asceticism, world-renuncia-
tion and self-mortification."[21] The right to develop one's aesthetic
sensibilities so that one can appreciate beauty in all its forms, and the
right to enjoy what God has created for the nurture of humankind, are
thus rooted in the life-affirming vision of the Qur'an. [22]

The right to leave one's homeland under oppressive conditions. According to Qur'anic teaching, a Muslim's ultimate loyalty is to God
and not to any place. The Prophet Muhammad migrated from his
birthplace, Mecca, to Medina in order to fulfill his prophetic mission.
This event (*Hijrah*) has great historical and spiritual significance for
Muslims who are called upon to move away from their place of origin
if it becomes an abode of evil where they cannot fulfill their obligations to God or to establish justice.[23]

The right to "the Good Life." The Qur'an upholds the right of a human being not only to life but to "the good life." This good life, made
up of many elements, becomes possible only when a human being is
living in a just environment. According to Qur'anic teaching, justice is
a prerequisite for peace, and peace is a prerequisite for human development. In a just society, all the earlier-mentioned human rights may
be exercised without difficulty. In such a society, other basic rights,
such as the right to a secure place of residence, the right to the protection of one's personal possessions, the right to the protection of one's
covenants, and the right to move freely, also exist.[24]

Muslim women partake of all the rights that have been mentioned
above. In addition, women are the subject of much particular concern
in the Qur'an. However, a review of Muslim history and culture brings
to light many areas in which—Qur'anic teachings notwithstanding—
women continued to be subjected to diverse forms of oppression and
injustice, often in the name of Islam.

Although the Qur'an, because of its protective attitude toward all
downtrodden and oppressed classes of people, appears to be weighted
in many ways in favor of women, many of its women-related teachings
have been used in patriarchal Muslim societies against, rather than for,
women. Muslim societies in general appear to be far more concerned
with trying to control women's bodies and sexuality than with wom-
en's human rights. Many Muslims, when they speak of human rights,

either do not speak of women's rights at all[25] or are mainly concerned with how a woman's chastity may be protected.[26]

WOMEN IN ISLAM: QUR'ANIC IDEALS VERSUS MUSLIM REALITIES

Despite the fact that the Qur'an is particularly solicitous about women's well-being and development, women have been the target of the most serious violations of human rights that occur in Muslim societies in general. In particular, attention needs to be drawn to the discrepancies between Qur'anic ideals, on the one hand, and, on the other, Muslim practice with regard to the following women and women-related issues.

Attitude toward female children. Muslim societies tend to discriminate against female children from the moment of birth. It is customary among Muslims to regard a son as a gift, and a daughter as a trial, from God. Therefore, the birth of a son is an occasion for celebration while the birth of a daughter calls for commiseration, if not lamentation. Here, it may be mentioned that although Muslims say with great pride that Islam abolished female infanticide, one of the most common crimes in many Muslim countries is the murder of women by their male relatives. These so-called honor-killings are frequently used to camouflage other kinds of crime.

Marriage. Much Qur'anic legislation is aimed at protecting the rights of women in the context of marriage.[27] However, many girls are married when they are still minors and do not understand that marriage in Islam is a contract and that women, as well as men, have the right to negotiate the terms of this contract. The Qur'anic description of man and woman in marriage—"They are your garments, And you are their garments"[28]—implies closeness, mutuality, and equality. But Muslim societies in general have never regarded men and women as equal, particularly in the context of marriage. The husband, in fact, is regarded not only as the wife's *majazi khuda* (god in earthly form) but also as her gateway to heaven or hell and the arbiter of her final destiny. That such an idea can exist within the framework of Islam—which, in theory, considers the deification of any human being as *shirk* (polytheism), regarded by the Qur'an as the one unforgivable sin, and which rejects the idea that there can be any intermediary between a believer and God, represents both a profound irony and a great tragedy.

Marital problems and divorce. While the Qur'an provides for just arbitration in case a marriage runs into problems, it also makes provisions for what we today call a "no-fault" divorce and does not make any adverse judgments about divorce.[29] The Qur'anic prescription, "Either live together in kindness or separate in kindness," preserves the spirit of amity and justice in the context of both marriage and divorce. In Muslim societies, however, divorce has been made extremely difficult for women, both legally and through social penalties.

Child rearing and child custody. In the context of child rearing, the Qur'an states clearly that the divorced parents of a minor child must decide by mutual consultation how the child is to be raised and that they must not use the child to exploit each other.[30] However, in Muslim societies, divorced women who have children are often subjected to great exploitation, losing the right to the custody of both boys (generally at age 7) and girls (generally at age 12). It is difficult to imagine an act of greater cruelty than depriving a mother of her children simply because she is divorced.

Polygamy. Polygamy was intended by the Qur'an to be for the protection of orphans and widows.[31] In practice, however, it has been widely misused and made into a sword of Damocles that is a constant threat to women.

Inheritance. One of the most revolutionary steps taken by the Qur'an for the empowerment of women was to give women the right of inheritance. Few women in the world have had this right until the modern period.

According to Qur'anic prescription, not only could women inherit on the death of a close relative; they could also receive bequests or gifts during the lifetime of a benevolent caretaker. In general, however, Muslim societies have disapproved of the idea of giving wealth to a woman in preference to a man, even when she is economically disadvantaged or in need. The intent of the Qur'anic laws of inheritance was to give all members of a family—including women as daughters, mothers, sisters, and wives—a share in the inheritance so that the family wealth was equitably distributed among all the legal heirs. The fact that women—to whom no financial responsibility was ascribed—

were given a share indicates the concern of the Qur'an to give women financial autonomy and security. However, Muslims have used the un-equal share accorded to men and women in some (not all) cases (e. g., in the case of a son, whose share is twice that of a daughter) to argue that men are worth twice as much as women. A profound rereading of the Qur'anic texts relating to inheritance is very important for com-bating the discriminatory attitude toward women in the context of in-heritance that is widely prevalent in Muslim societies.

Segregation and "veiling" (purdah). Although the purpose of the Qur'anic legislation dealing with women's dress and conduct[32] was to make it safe for women to go about their daily business—which in-cluded the right to engage in gainful activity (as testified to by *An-Nisa'* 4: 32)—without fear of sexual molestation or harassment, Muslim so-cieties have segregated women or put them behind shrouds or veils and locked doors on the pretext of protecting their chastity. Among the changes brought about in the Muslim world by the onset of mo-dernity has been the appearance in public space of an increasing num-ber of women. The crossing by many women of the traditional boundary between the home and the world has, in fact, been a critical factor in bringing about the "Islamization" of a number of contempo-rary Muslim societies. Conservative Muslims have made massive ef-forts to keep women segregated by insisting that a chaste Muslim woman ought to wear the chador (a large shawl covering the body) and stay within the *chardewari* (four walls) of the home. They have also insisted that a woman's Muslim identity is determined largely if not solely by whether she covers her hair or not.

The debate between "veiled" and "unveiled" women rages through-out the Muslim communities of the world and has split Muslim wom-en from Turkey to Indonesia, as well as in the Western world, into rival camps. Here, it is important to mention that according to the Qur'an,[33] confinement to the home was not the norm for chaste Mus-lim women but, rather, the punishment for unchaste women. Further, it needs to be noted that the history of veiling pre-dates Islam and is profoundly linked with discriminatory ideas regarding women found in the Jewish and Christian traditions.[34] The historical context of the Qur'anic prescriptions relating to *hijab* (literally, "curtain"), which refers to both seclusion and veiling, also needs to be understood.[35]

Special focus needs to be put on the issue of segregation and *purdah* due to its multifaceted and vast sociological impact on the lives of millions of Muslim women.

Family planning. An overview of the sources of the Islamic tradition shows that there is much support for family planning within the religious and ethical framework as well as the legal and philosophical literature of Islam. Despite this fact, in practice, family planning programs continue to fare badly in most Muslim societies, where the birth rate is among the highest in the world. This is due in part to the fact that masses of Muslim women do not have adequate access to reliable means of contraception. But it is also due in significant measure to the widespread influence of conservative Muslims who proclaim from public platforms, as well as preach from mosque pulpits, that family planning is against Islam. Here it is appropriate to observe that the three Muslim countries in which family planning programs have done better—Indonesia, Bangladesh, and Iran—are those in which the religious leaders and preachers have supported family planning. An examination of both the normative literature of Islam and the sociological factors that are relevant to the issue of family planning in contemporary Muslim societies provides strong evidence why the right to use contraception should be regarded as a fundamental human right, especially in the case of disadvantaged Muslim women whose lives are scarred by grinding poverty and massive illiteracy.

Other theological issues. Other theological issues that are important in the context of gender justice and equity in Islam relate to statements widely made in Muslim societies to foreclose any discussion on the subject of women's equality with men. Among such statements are the following: (1) the evidence of one man is equal to that of two women; (2) a woman's blood-fine is one-half of a man's blood-fine;[36] (3) a woman is deficient in reason whereas a man is not; (4) a woman is less religious than a man in prayer or worship (because of menstruation, childbirth, etc.); (5) righteous men will be rewarded by beautiful companions in the hereafter, but no such reward exists for righteous women; (6) a woman cannot be a prophet. None of those statements is supported by an accurate reading of the Qur'anic text. Rather, they are grounded in a patriarchal culture in which women are regarded as inferior to men, who alone are regarded as being fully human.

Other issues relating to women's health and well-being. The negative ideas and attitudes regarding women that have become incorporated in the Islamic tradition have had a profound impact on the physical, psychological, and emotional health of Muslim women. There is, therefore, urgent need to investigate the relationship or linkage between the state of physical, mental, and emotional well-being of Muslim women and the theological and cultural framework within which they live. In particular, it is important to examine the way in which masses of Muslim women perceive themselves or why so many Muslim women have low self-esteem and put such little value on their life or its quality.

CURRENT DISCOURSE ON MUSLIM WOMEN'S RIGHTS: A CASE STUDY—PAKISTAN

The subject of Muslim women's rights is generating more discussion in the contemporary Muslim world than perhaps any other subject. The case of Pakistan well illustrates the polarization of views that characterizes the on-going discourse.

Two Opposing Mindsets

The discourse on women's rights is dominated by two highly vocal and visible groups that represent opposing mindsets. In some ways both of these mindsets can be described as "extremist." The first mindset is of persons who consider themselves the custodians of "Islam," which they generally define in narrowly construed literalistic and legalistic terms. The second mindset is of persons who consider themselves the guardians of "human rights," which they believe are incompatible with religion, particularly Islam.

A review of Pakistan's history shows that "religious" extremists have generally opposed any critical review or reform of traditional attitudes and practices that have become associated with popular Muslim culture. In particular, they have been opposed to any changes in the traditional roles of women and have regarded the movement for women's rights as a great threat to the integrity and solidarity of the Muslim family system.

Averse in general to "modernity"—which they identify largely with the so-called Westernization of Muslim societies—the religious extremists have raised a red flag and cried out that "the integrity of the Islamic way of life" is under assault each time any government has taken any step to address the issue of gender inequality or discrimination against women.

While extremism is most often associated with the so-called religious right referred to above, it is also found in the utterances and actions of those who regard religion, especially Islam, negatively. In asserting that Islam and human rights are mutually exclusive, a number of human rights advocates adopt a position that is untenable on both theoretical and pragmatic grounds. The Qur'an strongly affirms all the fundamental human rights. In pragmatic terms, it is evident that Muslims generally—including the vast majority of Pakistanis— are strong believers in God and Islam, regardless of how they express or enact their beliefs. The insistence by "antireligious" advocates of human rights that Islam should not be part of the ongoing discourse on human rights in Pakistan is therefore vacuous. Whether those advocates like to acknowledge it or not, Islam defines the identity and day-to-day reality of millions of Pakistanis and is already—and inevitably—a part of this discourse.

Creation of a Third Option—The New Paradigm

Vocal and visible as they are, the extremists in Pakistan constitute a small percentage of the country's total population. The vast majority of Pakistanis are "middle-of-the-road" people who neither subscribe to nor support extremism. While they have a strong Muslim identity and their faith is very important to them, they also aspire to be part of the modern world through acquiring education, awareness of contemporary values, and the means to have what the Greeks called "the good life." In other words, they want both *deen* (religion) and *dunya* (the world). This is a position supported by Qur'anic teaching and the Prophetic example, which describes Islam as a religion of balance and moderation stressing the interconnected and complementary nature of various spheres of life.

It is a matter of utmost gravity that, in Pakistan, the discourse on Islam has been hijacked by religious extremists and the discourse on human rights has been hijacked by antireligious extremists. It is vitally important to broaden the discourse on both Islam and human rights to include a third option. This means the creation of a new discourse, or an alternative paradigm that is grounded in the ethical principles of the Qur'an and relates to the beliefs as well as the aspirations of moderate, middle-of-the-road Pakistanis.

Islam is undoubtedly the sustaining factor in the lives of millions of Muslims—including Pakistanis—many of whom live in conditions of great hardship, suffering, or oppression. It can easily become a source of empowerment for them if they begin to see that they have been given a large number of rights, not by any human agency but by God. Once the masses that constitute "the silent majority" of Pakistanis become conscious of their God-given right to actualize their human potential to the fullest, they can be mobilized to participate in building a dynamic and democratic society. But to make this happen, a new perspective on human rights (including women's rights)—one grounded in normative Islamic ideas of universalism, rationalism, moderation, social justice, and compassion—must be disseminated as widely as possible.

CONCLUSION

Although violations of women's rights are widespread in the Muslim world, it must be borne in mind that the Qur'an does not discriminate against women. Not only does the Qur'an emphasize that righteousness is identical in the case of both men and women, but it clearly and consistently affirms women's equality with men and their fundamental right to actualize the human potential that they share equally with men. In fact, when seen through a nonpatriarchal lens, the Qur'an goes beyond egalitarianism. It exhibits particular solicitude toward women, as it also does toward other classes of disadvantaged persons. Further, it provides particular safeguards for protecting women's special sexual/biological functions such as carrying, delivering, suckling, and rearing offspring.

God, who speaks through the Qur'an, is characterized by justice, and it is stated clearly in the Qur'an that God can never be guilty of *zulm* (unfairness, tyranny, oppression, or wrongdoing). Hence, gender injustice cannot be legitimized with reference to any Qur'anic text. The goal of Qur'anic Islam is to establish peace, which can only exist within a just environment. Here it is of importance to note that there is more Qur'anic legislation pertaining to the establishment of justice in the context of family relationships than on any other subject. This points to the assumption implicit in much Qur'anic legislation, namely, that if human beings can learn to order their homes justly so that the rights of all who live within—children, women, men—are safeguarded, then they can also order their society and the world at large justly.

Many in the West are as unaware of the critical thinking that has been going on in a number of Muslim societies as they are of the normative teachings of Islam. It is very important for dialogue-oriented Westerners to know that liberal and progressive Muslims have been engaged in a long struggle to reform both Islamic tradition and Muslim societies from within.

Between 1850 and 1950 there was a renaissance of critical thinking in a number of Muslim countries. During this time—the final phase of colonialism in much of the Muslim world—the issue of political independence was a paramount concern for many Muslim thinkers. Like the great nineteenth-century Muslim reformist and political activist Jamal al-Din al-Afghani, they sought to identify the internal weaknesses of Muslim societies that had made possible their colonization by Western powers and to find ways of overcoming them. Realizing the negative impact on the lives of masses of Muslims of fossilized traditions sanctified by reference to religion or culture, many significant thinkers of this period reached the conclusion that Muslims had to "go back to the Qur'an" and "go forward with *ijtihad*" (independent reasoning). In other words, to become free and strong people, Muslims had to discover the universal ethical principles highlighted by the Qur'an and apply them by means of their rational understanding to real-life situations.

In recent times there has been much fear in the West that Muslims want to create "theocratic" societies in which the Shari'a would be the supreme law. There has also been much discussion in Muslim societies about what the Shari'a stands for. Here, it may be useful to note that the term *Shari'a* comes from the root *Shar'a*, which means "to open, to become clear." E. W. Lane points out in his monumental *Arabic-English Lexicon* that, according to the authors of authoritative Arabic lexicons—the *Taj al-`Arus*, the *Tadheeb*, and the *Misbah*—Arabs do not apply the term *shari-at* to "any but (a watering place) such as is permanent and apparent to the eye, like the water of a river, not water from which one draws with the well-rope."[37] A modern lexicon, *Lughat ul Qur'an*, states that *Shari'a* refers to a straight and clear path as well as to a watering place where both humans and animals come to drink water, provided the source of water is a flowing stream or river.[38] It is not a little ironic that the term, which has the idea of fluidity and mobility as part of its very structure, should have become the symbol of rigid and unchanging laws to so many Muslims in the world.

That the Shari'a has played a pivotal role in Islamic history as a means of bringing diverse groups of Muslims within a single legal religious framework is beyond dispute. However, in my judgment, the assertion that one is a Muslim only if one accepts the Shari'a as binding upon oneself, and, further, accepts it as divine, transcendent, and eternal, needs to be subjected to rigorous moral and intellectual scrutiny.

Being a Muslim is dependent essentially only upon one belief: belief in God, universal creator and sustainer who sends revelation for the guidance of humanity. Believing in God and God's revelation to and through the Prophet Muhammad, preserved in the Qur'an, is not, however, identical with accepting the Shari'a as binding upon oneself. As Wilfred Cantwell Smith has remarked insightfully, "A true Muslim...is not a man who believes in Islam—especially Islam in history; but one who believes in God and is committed to the revelation through His Prophet."[39]

Today it is vitally important to remember that, for Muslims, God and God's word alone is divine and that deification of Muslim tradition and law runs counter to the fundamental teaching of Islam. In this context it is good to hear the refreshing voice of Muhammad Iqbal, modern Islam's most outstanding thinker and visionary. Iqbal was a passionate advocate for *ijtihad*, which he insightfully called "the principle of movement in Islam." In his lecture on ijtihad Iqbal says:

> I know the Ulema[40] of Islam claim finality for the popular schools of Muslim Law, though they never found it possible to deny the theoretical possibility of a complete ijtihad. ... [41] For fear of... disintegration, the conservative thinkers of Islam focused all their efforts on the one point of preserving a uniform social life for the people by a jealous exclusion of all innovations in the law of Shari'ah as expounded by the early doctors of Islam. Their leading idea was social

order, and there is no doubt that they were partly right, because organization does to a certain extent counteract the forces of decay.
But they did not see, and our modern Ulema do not see, that the
ultimate fate of a people does not depend so much on organization
as on the worth and power of individual men. In an over-organized
society the individual is altogether crushed out of existence....[42]
The closing of the door of Ijtihad is pure fiction suggested partly by
the crystallization of legal thought in Islam, and partly by that intellectual laziness which, especially in a period of spiritual decay, turns
great thinkers into idols. If some of the later doctors have upheld
this fiction, modern Islam is not bound by this voluntary surrender
of intellectual independence....[43] Since things have changed and the
world of Islam is today confronted and affected by new forces set
free by the extraordinary development of human thought in all its
directions, I see no reason why this attitude (of the Ulema) should
be maintained any longer. Did the founders of our schools ever
claim finality for their reasonings and interpretations? Never. The
claim of the present generation of Muslim liberals to re-interpret
the foundational legal principles in the light of their own experience and altered conditions of modern life is, in my opinion, perfectly justified. The teaching of the Qur'an that life is a process of
progressive creation necessitates that each generation, guided but
unhampered by the work of its predecessors, should be permitted
to solve its own problems.[44]

In my judgment, the most important issue confronting the Muslim
ummah as a whole in the twenty-first century is that of gender equality and gender justice. The Islamic tradition, like the traditions of the
world's major religions, namely, Judaism, Christianity, Hinduism,
and Buddhism, developed in a patriarchal culture, one that was
male-centered and male-controlled. Today, women-related issues pertaining to various aspects of personal as well as social life lie at the
heart of much of the ferment or unrest that characterizes the Muslim
world in general.

Many of these issues are not new, but the manner in which they are
being debated today is new. Much of the ongoing debate has been generated by the enactment of manifestly anti-woman laws in a number
of Muslim countries. For instance, since the 1970s, many Pakistani

women have been jolted out of their "dogmatic slumber" by the enactment of laws such as the Hudood Ordinance (1979), the Law of Evidence (1984), and the Qisas and Diyat Ordinance (1990), which
discriminate against women in a blatant manner. These laws, which
pertain to women's testimony in cases regarding their own rape or regarding financial and other matters, and to blood money for women's
murder, aim at reducing the value and status of women systematically,
virtually mathematically, to less than that of men.

Having spent more than 30 years conducting research on women in
the Qur'an, I know that the Qur'an does not discriminate against
women. In fact, in view of their disadvantaged and vulnerable condition, it is highly protective of women's rights and interests. But this
does not change the fact that the way Islam has been practiced in most
Muslim societies for centuries has left millions of Muslim women with
battered bodies, minds, and souls.

Here it is appropriate to mention that some Muslim reformers in
the modern period have attached primary importance to the issue of
women's empowerment, which they have regarded as being pivotal to
the future of the Muslim ummah (or community). The classic works
on the rights of Muslim women by Mumtaz 'Ali (in India) and Qasim
Amin (in Egypt) were published more than a hundred years ago and
presented a compelling case for improving the status of women. A
number of contemporary liberal Muslim scholars who have been critical of cultural attitudes and practices that are detrimental to women
have also stressed the importance of recognizing and implementing
women's rights. The intellectual work being done to liberate women
from injustice and oppression is being supplemented on the ground by
numerous grassroots groups that are helping girls and women through
projects relating to literacy and education, health and family planning, economic and political development, protection from domestic
and social violence, and various other spheres of life.

Today, an increasing number of Muslims—especially those belonging to women's groups, youth groups, and a number of other grassroots groups—are realizing more and more that if the Muslim ummah
is to become worthy of being the khalifah of God on earth and is to
actualize its highest potential, it will have to make a strong commitment to establishing gender justice and gender equality in all spheres

of life. No society can claim to be truly Islamic unless it recognizes, in word and in deed, that man and woman are equal before God and that each has an equal right to develop his or her God-given capabilities to the fullest.

In Qur'anic terms, Islam represents the "middle way" between two extremes—it is the religion of moderation, of balance. Most Muslims, including Pakistanis, are not extremists, and many of them could be classified as "moderate," "liberal," or "progressive." If one recalls the history of the Muslims of the Indo-Pakistan-Bangladesh subcontinent in the one hundred years before the creation of Pakistan, the leaders who liberated the Muslims from the "yoke" of foreign domination, both political and intellectual, were the reformers (for instance, of the 'Aligarh movement from Syed Ahmed Khan to Allama Iqbal) and not the Revivalists who wanted to recreate the conditions prevailing in the mythic Golden Age of early Islam. Whereas the former recognized the urgent need to critique all of the negative elements that hampered the development of the Muslim community, the latter denied that there was anything wrong with the Muslim community and put the blame for all its weaknesses on others.

The best hope of liberating Pakistan and the rest of the Muslim world from extremists—whether religious or antireligious—is the emergence of an educated group of persons who understand Islam to be a religion of justice and compassion, of knowledge and reason, of openness and peace, and who believe that it is possible to build a justice-centered society within the ethical framework of the Qur'an, which is the Magna Carta of human rights.

While many in the West and in the Muslim world focus heavily on the damage done by the extremists, it should be borne in mind that it is the so-called enlightened Muslims who have for too long abdicated their responsibility to articulate their perspective. They have failed seriously in two ways. First, they have allowed the religious extremists to become sole spokespersons for Islam, to teach hatred and bigotry and violence in the name of a religion that is supposed to be a blessing for all humanity. Second, they have allowed the antireligious extremists who maintain that Islam and human rights are incompatible to hijack the human rights discourse and to monopolize the right and authority to speak about human rights. In my judgment, vocal as these two groups of extremists are, they do not represent mainstream Muslims, who are indeed "in the middle." It is the perspective represented by the moderate, liberal, and progressive Muslims who form "the silent majority" that now must be voiced.

History has brought us to a point where neither politically correct statements nor a superficial analysis of the serious problems of women in the Muslim world will suffice to change or even camouflage reality. Much hard work needs to be done to examine and understand the root causes of discrimination against girls and women in different Muslim societies through a systematic and scientific analysis of both theoretical and empirical data. Once the underlying factors have been correctly discerned, it will become possible to develop and implement plans and programs aimed at creating an environment that is just and compassionate and in which the human rights of every child, woman, and man are regarded as sacred.

The challenge before women in general, and Muslim women in particular, is to shift from the reactive mindset, in which women must assert their autonomy in the face of strong opposition from patriarchal structures and systems of thought and behavior, to a proactive mindset in which they can, finally, begin to speak of themselves as full and autonomous human beings. What do Muslim women—who along with Muslim men have been designated by the Qur'an as God's vicegerents on earth—understand to be the meaning of their lives? Reacting against the Western model of human liberation no longer suffices; a proactive orientation requires a positive formulation of one's goals and objectives. The critical issue on which Muslim women are called to reflect, with utmost seriousness, after the historic United Nations conferences of the 1990s, is: What kind of model of self-actualization can be developed within the framework of normative Islam that takes account of Qur'anic ideals as well as the realities of the contemporary Muslim world?

George Santayana remarked with acute insight that those who do not know their history are destined to repeat it. Until such time that the vast majority of Muslim women become aware of the religious ideas and attitudes that constitute the matrix in which their lives are rooted, it is not possible to usher in a new era and create a new history in which the Qur'anic vision of gender justice and equity becomes a reality.

Although the West constantly bemoans what it refers to as the "rise of Islamic fundamentalism," it does not extend significant recognition or support to progressive Muslims who are far more representative of "mainstream" modern Islam than either the religious or the antireligious extremists in the Muslim world. Even after the Iranian Revolution and the "Islamization" of an increasing number of Muslim societies, many Western analysts are still unable or unwilling to see Islam as a religion capable of being interpreted in a progressive way or being a source of liberation to Muslim peoples. An even deeper problem is their refusal to understand the pivotal role of Islam in the lives of Muslims, the vast majority of whom are "believers" rather than "unbelievers."

Compelled by facts of modern history, some social scientists in the West are now beginning to concede that Islam is one of the factors that needs to be considered—along with political, economic, ethnic, social, and other factors—in planning and evaluating development projects. This approach, although an improvement on the one that takes no account of religion at all, is still not adequate for understanding the issues of the Muslim world or finding ways to resolve them. Islam is not, in my judgment, simply one of the factors that has a decisive influence on the lives of Muslims. It is the matrix in which all other factors are grounded. I do not believe that any viable model of self-actualization can be constructed in Muslim societies, for women or men, that is outside the framework of normative Islam deriving from Qur'anic teachings and exemplified in the life of the Prophet of Islam. Nor do I believe that any profoundly meaningful or constructive dialogue can take place between "the World of Islam" and "the West" without a proper recognition of what Islam means to millions of Muslims.

Notes

[1] Thomas Aquinas, as quoted by E. W. Fernea in her presentation on "Roles of Women in Islam: Past and Present," at the Ta'ziyeh Conference held at Hartford Seminary, Hartford, Connecticut, May 2, 1988.

[2] Thomas Carlyle, "The Hero as Prophet. Mahomet: Islam," in *On Heroes, Hero-Worship and the Heroic in History* (New York: Dutton, 1964), 279.

[3] Reference here is to the Qur'an, *An-Najm* 53:42. The translation is by Muhammad Iqbal, *The Reconstruction of Religious Thought in Islam* (Lahore: Shaikh Muhammad Ashraf, 1971), 57.

[4] *Al-An'am* 6:151.

[5] *Al-Ma'idah* 5:32.

[6] *Al-Ma'idah* 5:8; *An-Nisa'* 4:36.

[7] *An-Nur* 24:2.

[8] *An-Nisa'i* 4:25; *Al-Ahzab* 33:30.

[9] *Ash-Shura* 42:21.

[10] *Yusuf* 12:40.

[11] *Ash-Shura* 42:38.

[12] K. M. Ishaque, "Islamic Law: Its Ideals and Principles," in *The Challenge of Islam*, ed. A. Gauhar (London: Islamic Council of Europe, 1980), 157.

[13] *Al-Baqarah* 2:256.

[14] *An-Nisa'* 4:135.

[15] *Al-Baqarah* 2:282.

[16] *An-Nur* 24:27–28; *Al-Ahzab* 33:53; *Al-Hujurat* 49:12.

[17] *Al-Hujurat* 49:11-12.

[18] *An-Nur* 24:15–19.

[19] *Al-An'am* 6:165; *Al-Mulk* 67:15.

[20] *An-Nisa'* 4:32.

[21] Muhammad Asad, *The Message of the Qur'an* (Gibraltar: Dar Al-Andalus, 1980), 207, footnote 24.

[22] *Al-A'raf* 7:32.

[23] *An-Nisa'* 4:97–100.

[24] *Al-Baqarah* 2:229; *Al-'Imran* 3:17, 77; *Al-Ma'idah* 5:42–48; *Al-Mulk* 67:15.

[25] For example, R. A. Jullundhri, "Human Rights in Islam," in *Understanding Human Rights,* ed. A. D. Falconer (Dublin: Irish School of Ecumenics, 1980).

[26] For example, A. A. Maududi, *Human Rights in Islam* (Lahore: Islamic Publications, 1977).

[27] *Al-Baqarah* 2:187; *An-Nisa'* 4:4, 19; *Al-A'raf* 7:189; *Al-Tawbah* 9:71; *An-Nur* 24:33; *Ar-Rum* 30:21.

[28] *Al-Baqarah* 2:187.

[29] *Al-Baqarah* 2:231–241.

[30] *Al-Baqarah* 2:233.

[31] *An-Nisa'* 4:2–3.

[32] *An-Nur* 24:30–31; *Al-Ahzab* 33:59.

[33] *An-Nisa'* 4:15.

[34] For instance, the following words of St. Paul have had a formative impact on the Christian tradition: "Christ is the source of every man, man is the source of woman, and God is the source of Christ. For a man to pray or prophesy with his head covered is a sign of disrespect to his source. For a woman, however, it is a sign of disrespect to her source if she prays or prophesies unveiled; she might as well have her hair cut off. If a woman is ashamed to have her hair cut off or shaved, she ought to wear a veil. A man should certainly not cover his head, since he is the image of God and reflects God's glory, but woman is the reflection of man's glory. For man did not come from woman; and man was not created for the sake of woman, but woman was created for the sake of man" (1 Corinthians 11:3–9), cited in *Biblical Affirmations of Woman*, ed. Leonard Swidler (Philadelphia: Westminster Press, 1979), 33.

[35] Fatima Mernissi has given the historical background of the "descent" of "hijab" in her book *The Veil and the Male Elite: A Feminist Interpretation of Women's Rights in Islam*, trans. Mary Jo Lakeland (Reading, Mass.: Addison-Wesley, 1991).

[36] A blood-fine, or blood money (*diyat*), is the compensation paid to the closest relatives of someone killed as a settlement to prevent further bloodshed over the killing.—Ed.

[37] E. W. Lane, *Arabic-English Lexicon*, Book I, Part 4 (London: William and Norgate, 1863), 1535.

[38] G. A. Parwez, *Lughat ul Qur'an*, vol. 2 (Lahore: Idara Tulu' e Islam, 1960), 941–944.

[39] Wilfred Cantwell Smith, *Islam in Modern History* (Princeton, N.J.: Princeton University Press, 1957), 146.

[40] *Ulema*: scholars of Islamic law and jurisprudence.

[41] Iqbal, *Reconstruction of Religious Thought in Islam*, 168.

[42] Ibid., 151.

[43] Ibid., 178.

[44] Ibid., 168.

CHAPTER FIVE

MINORITY RIGHTS IN ISLAM
FROM *DHIMMI* TO CITIZEN

Recep Senturk

Until the nineteenth century, at least a dozen legal traditions were practiced in the Ottoman Empire: five non-Islamic (Jewish, Armenian, Orthodox, Catholic, and Copt) along with four Sunni (Hanafi, Shafi'i, Maliki, and Hanbali) and several Shiite (such as Zaydiyya and Jafariyya). During the late nineteenth century, under European influence, secular law (such as international commercial courts) was also added to the Ottoman legal system. Each community produced and practiced its own canon law, thereby contributing to the diversity of legal discourse. The state did not produce any of these laws nor did it single out any of them as the official law of the state; instead, Muslim and non-Muslim civil groups crafted them. The state stood in equal distance to all and equally respected each one.

By contrast, at the turn of the twentieth century, which was a period of intense modernization, only one official law was practiced in the empire. The first Ottoman constitution was declared on December 23, 1876. It was also the first constitution in any Muslim country. After a general election—the first in Islamic history—the first Ottoman parliament, summoned under the constitution in March 1877, worked for the enactment of Islamic law as the official law to be practiced throughout the empire by all subjects.[1] It was the first enactment of Islamic law by the state, marking the end of the traditional pluralist legal system.

Increasing centralization of state power and bureaucracy during the nineteenth century created a need for uniformity in the legal system. The trend initially emerged in Europe, which the Ottomans emulated while trying to modernize their state and legal system. Consequently, the universal application of Islamic law was a short-lived experience in the Ottoman Empire. After the collapse of the empire, the new Turkish republic went even further in the process of Westernization and adopted a secular legal system, a patchwork of quick translations from the legal codes of several Western countries.[2] At every stage of this process, the identity of minorities and their rights were redefined as a result of the reconfiguration of the relationship between law and religion to facilitate further control of society by the state. With the benefit of hindsight, this was a failed strategy with numerous unintended consequences.

This chapter describes three stages in the history of Islamic law, deriving for the most part from the Ottoman and Turkish experience, as it bears upon minority rights: (1) the classical period, from the seventh century until the end of the eighteenth century; (2) Islamic modernization, from the beginning of the nineteenth to the first quarter of the twentieth century; and (3) secularization, or separation of law and religion, from the first quarter of the twentieth century until the present. This broad and imprecise periodization is derived from the Ottoman and Turkish history and its unique experience of secularism. Consequently, it may not be applicable to all Muslim countries. The purpose of this analysis, however, is not to provide a historical survey of the Muslim world as a whole, but to demonstrate the fluidity of the concept of minority and the rights accorded to it within the lengthy and diverse history of Islamic tradition. The primary focus will be on the Ottoman Empire and Turkey, but will also draw on the experience of the broader Muslim world and its relations with Europe and the United States.

ISLAMIC LEGAL TRADITION

Islamic legal tradition is best understood as part of Western legal tradition, as is the religion of Islam.[3] Indeed, the history of law in Europe and the history of law in the Muslim world have been closely intertwined since the Middle Ages, with striking parallels at each stage of major transformation in the Islamic and European legal tradition.

Under classical Islamic law, both Muslim and non-Muslim minorities enjoyed a considerable degree of freedom. This situation produced a state of legal pluralism that embraced Muslims and non-Muslims with divergent perspectives on law. The situation was termed "Open Law," meaning a legal system that allowed multiple legal systems and discourse communities to coexist peacefully within a society. The governing principle in that period was, "A legal opinion cannot nullify another one."[4] Classical Islamic legal discourse produced two sets of rules, namely those aimed at regulating the internal affairs of the Muslim community and those aimed at regulating the affairs among different religious communities as well as between non-Muslims and Muslims. These rules derived from principles that all legal traditions unanimously accepted. Muslim jurists from the classical era defined these principles as *al-daruriyyat al-shar'iyyah*, "axioms of law," because they were taken as given without dispute. Islamic law did not produce laws to regulate the internal affairs of non-Muslim communities, but non-Muslims were allowed to apply to a Muslim court if the conflicting parties were agreeable.

Under this system, each religious community had considerable autonomy to regulate its own internal affairs in accordance with its canon law. This right was granted to all religious communities, including Buddhists, Hindus, Zoroastrians, and Sabians, along with Jews and Christians. The latter two were called the People of the Book to indicate the intimate connection of their religions with Islam. It is a common misconception that Islamic law granted freedom of religion only to the People of the Book. A brief review of Islamic classical legal texts[5] and their practice, particularly in Iran and India,[6] demonstrates that the opposite was the case. Furthermore, each Muslim school of law (*madhhab*) had the right to practice Islam in accordance with its own interpretation.[7] As new legal discourse communities emerged among Muslims and non-Muslims, the Open Law approach allowed their participation in the plurality of legal systems under Islamic rule.

Among the students of that period, those who compare Islamic law with minority rights in Muslim and non-Muslim societies during the Middle Ages find Islamic law progressive.[8] Yet those who look at Islamic law retrospectively from the vantage point of contemporary standards of minority rights find it restrictive or oppressive.[9] The former strategy is adopted by apologists while the latter strategy is adopted by opponents of Islam. In reality, both perspectives are selective—partial and one-sided—and tell only half of the story. The analysis that follows, in contrast, uses an historically grounded, balanced, and critical approach.

The question of whether Islam has already provided or can ever provide equal rights for minorities within a democratic and pluralistic system is related to the broader discussion of the relationship between religion and law: can any religion do so? Moral and legal justification of the rights of minorities is a prerequisite for the sustainable protection of minority rights within a pluralistic and democratic system of governance. Such a justification is currently provided either by a secular ideology or by a religion, with a wide gap in between the two sources. The official discourse in modern democracies is usually characterized by a secular vision, while the more popular discourse is characterized by a religious vision. Is this gap logically required because the secular and religious justifications are mutually exclusive? Or is it possible to ground pluralism and democracy simultaneously on both religious and secular ideas?

Traditionally, the answer has been either secularism or religion. Recently a trend has emerged, however, that aims to construct a new framework that would allow combining secular and religious viewpoints on pluralism and democracy.[10] If there is nothing in the religious and secular approaches to make them mutually exclusive on their view as to the inviolability of the rights of others, then it seems plausible to allow them to work together with a synergy in promoting pluralism and democracy. With the resurgence of religion everywhere in the world, such an approach may better serve mutual respect.

The prevailing conviction is that religion cannot safeguard or respect the rights of minorities because these rights can be guaranteed only from a nonreligious or secular legal perspective. This argument is based on the claim that only secular law can be neutral and equally distanced from various belief systems and faith communities. The fact that all religions have often been misused to justify oppression of religious minorities supports this claim. Furthermore, religion has also been misused to justify oppression of other groups such as women, racial minorities, and colonized people. However, this view suffers from one-sidedness because history also shows that the same religions have contributed to the emancipation of minorities, if not to their final deliverance from oppression. For instance, the civil rights movement in America was led by Christian religious leaders. The Jews were given sanctuary by the caliph in Istanbul after their flight from Spain. Likewise, secular ideologies, such as nationalism and communism, have been used by some of their followers to justify oppression of minorities. Consequently, the connection between a particular type of culture, religious or secular, and respect for, or disregard of, minority rights is not straightforward. To clarify the relationship between the two requires a balanced, comprehensive, and deliberative approach.

Therefore, I will look at the question of minority rights in Islamic law from this perspective and will explore the possibility of bridging the present gap between secular (rational) and religious (scriptural) approaches to the inviolability of the other. Islamic jurisprudence provides a framework that can be used, as an example, to demonstrate that secular and religious reasoning in legal matters are not mutually exclusive. Rather, if properly bridged, they affirm each other.

I will also demonstrate how minority rights in Islamic law are grounded on the principle of *adamiyyah* (humanity), which entitles a human being to *dhimmah*, the right to legal personhood with accountability and inviolability. In doing so, I will use the works of the universalistic school of Muslim jurists from the classical period and will compare those views with the views of the communalistic school of the same period. I will also build upon the Ottoman legal reforms from the nineteenth century. I will use these two precedents at the conceptual and practical levels to demonstrate how Islamic law and the present universalistic approaches to human and minority rights can be bridged by exposing the commonalities between them—commonalities that are hardly known today to the proponents on either side.

ISLAMIC LAW AND MINORITY RIGHTS: INDIVIDUAL AND COMMUNAL

Islamic law approaches minority rights at two levels: individual and communal. The individual minority person is called *dhimmi*; the minority group is called *millah*.[11] A dhimmi may be defined as a person with accountability and inviolability, while a *millah*, or *millet*, is a religious community or a nation united around a religious identity and discourse. At both levels, minorities are granted "human" rights and "constitutional" rights. Human rights are universal and therefore do not vary from individual to individual or from community to community.

The latter group, the constitutional rights, may vary from group to group or from individual to individual. No matter how autonomous one is, the individual is always seen as embedded in the network of social relations in the context of which rights and duties are negotiated and determined. The emphasis on *adamiyyah* may be interpreted as emphasis on the autonomy of the individual. Because of the prevalence of the nation-state model during the late nineteenth century, Ottoman reforms concerning the status of minorities in Islamic law dismantled the traditional millet system. The result was a complete reform of Islamic law based on equal citizenship for all individuals, who no longer needed their religious community and leaders in their interaction with the political authority.

THE CONTEST OVER THE RIGHTS OF MINORITIES IN CLASSICAL ISLAMIC LAW

Jurists adopt divergent views on why minorities should be granted rights. Is it because of their humanity, or because of their citizenship? There are contradicting and evolving views advocated by jurists from the classical and modern periods. The cleavage between universalist and communalist jurists can be observed in all major legal traditions, including Islamic law. The former group believes that human beings, be they from the majority or the minority, are entitled to rights by virtue of their humanity. In contrast, the latter group is concerned only with the rights of the citizens of their state, usually called a nation, or with the members of their religious or ethnic community. The same structure can also be observed in Islamic law.

The cleavage between universal and communal perspectives in Islamic law is important for our concerns here.[12] The universalist school grounded human rights on humanity, *adamiyyah,* and thus advocated equal rights for all human beings regardless of their inherited and innate qualities such as class, race, color, language, religion, and ethnicity. This view was first formulated by Abu Hanifa (699–767 CE) in the following precept: Inviolability is due to all human beings by virtue of their humanity.[13]

In contrast, the communalist school did not accept universally granted human rights. Instead, it advocated civil rights, or constitutional rights granted to citizens by virtue of their citizenship. Their view is summarized in the following precept: Inviolability is due by virtue of faith or treaty.[14]

A similar tension is observable in Western legal history. Article 6 of the United Nations Charter stipulates: "Everyone has the right to recognition everywhere as a person before the law." This statement should be seen as a culmination of lengthy debates and conflicts in human history. Before this declaration, some segments of populations in the West, especially non-citizens and minorities, did not have the right to personhood. Right to personhood entitles one to have rights and responsibilities. Without it, human beings cannot bear rights and duties; in that case, they are treated as property or outcasts, but not as human beings with moral capacity.

In different periods of Western history, minorities were denied personhood, and they were dehumanized in order to justify their deprivation of personhood. Article 6 of the United Nations Charter aimed to end such discriminatory practices. Among the most well-known cases are colonized peoples, racial minorities such as African-Americans in the United States before the civil rights movement, Jews in Europe prior to the Jewish Emancipation, and women until the twentieth century.

PERSONHOOD IN ISLAM

The right to personhood is central to the understanding of the concept of the rights of minorities. In classical Islamic jurisprudence, as related earlier, the term *dhimmah* means accountability and inviolability, which is usually termed personhood in modern legal discourse.[15] Moral, religious, and legal accountability requires one to have dhimmah. If one has dhimmah, one can bear rights and responsibilities. Dhimmah distinguishes human beings from animals because humans are responsible for their actions. Having dhimmah is thus a privilege that entitles one to be a full member of society. Accountability before the law is a prerequisite for membership in society, which comes with a right to complete inviolability.

Dhimmah is also commonly understood as "protection," "treaty" (*'ahd*), and "peace" (*sulh*) because it is a treaty that puts non-Muslims under the protection of Muslims. Thus, "This is in his dhimmah" means that a person is accountable to the law or is under its protection. This accountability may be based on a written contract or a general law.

Islamic jurisprudence stipulates that dhimmah is what makes a person responsible for the consequences of his actions; because he has personhood, others can hold him liable for his deeds and demand that he fulfill his duties—which are their rights. Yet it is unanimously accepted that "one's dhimmah is originally clear of charges" (*al-Asl fi al-dhimmah al-bara'ah*) unless a charge is proven beyond doubt by evidence. This principle is interpreted as "one is innocent unless proven otherwise." According to this principle, no one can be held accountable unless there is clear evidence to the contrary. In other words, the burden of proof is on the claimant.

In conjunction with this issue, there is a conceptual debate between universalist and communalist jurists regarding who has dhimmah and on what grounds. This question has divided Muslim jurists. Some have claimed that dhimmah is a birthright and that people have dhimmah after conception by virtue of being human.[16] Others have contended that dhimmah is a gained right and that people obtain it by virtue of their citizenship. The non-Muslim individual who has a right to personhood is called dhimmi, while their community as a whole is called *ahl al-dhimmah*, which literally means "people with accountability and inviolability." The following citation from the prominent Hanafi jurist Sarakhsi (d. 1090 CE) succinctly elucidates this perspective:

> Upon creating human beings, God graciously bestowed upon them intelligence and the capability to carry responsibilities and rights (*dhimmah*, personhood). This was to make them ready for duties and rights determined by God. Then He granted them the right to inviolability, freedom, and property to let them continue their lives so that they can perform the duties they have shouldered. Then these rights to carry responsibility and enjoy rights, freedom, and property exist with a human being when he is born. The insane/child and the sane/adult are the same concerning these rights. This is how the proper personhood is given to him when he is born for God to charge him with the rights and duties when he is born. In this regard, the insane/child and sane/adult are equal.[17]

The Universalistic School

According to the universalistic school, all human beings have dhimmah by virtue of their humanity. The term *ahl al-dhimmah* is therefore literally true for all human beings around the globe because all people are born with dhimmah. Therefore, dhimmah may be called a birthright or a natural right. The fact that non-Muslim minorities are conventionally called so means nothing other than reiterating and affirming with a written contract that non-Muslims are equal with Muslims in enjoying this right. It indicates that non-Muslim minorities also have the right to legal personhood and that they *acknowledge* their accountability. It may be seen as a declaration of the equality in that aspect between Muslims and non-Muslims. Other non-Muslims, without a treaty with Muslim authority, have to officially acknowledge and register that they accept their accountability and liability before the law for their actions.

From this perspective, the compact of dhimmah is merely an act of acknowledgment by both sides about their rights and duties. This is because non-Muslims are already granted all the rights they may possibly have by virtue of their humanity, and thus signing a treaty with Muslims is not going to bring them new rights. However, the act of dhimmah serves as a confirmation of those rights and duties by both parties. It follows from the above principle that dhimmah cannot be repelled under any condition by any authority, be it either religious or political.

The Islamic discourse on rights is characterized by multiplexity and multiplicity. It is multiplex because it distinguishes between two levels: human rights and constitutional rights. The former are called "axiomatic rights" (*daruriyyat*), while the latter are divided into two categories—*hajiyyat* (requirements) and *tahsiniyyat* (improvements).[18] The discourse is universal at the first level, which is the level of universal human rights; but on the second level, which is the level of constitutional rights, it allows for diversity based on the culture and religion of the minorities.

The universalistic school sees no difference between Muslims and non-Muslims as far as human rights are concerned. The same is true between citizens of an Islamic state and others because human rights are not granted on the basis of citizenship. These basic rights include the right to life, property, freedom of religion, freedom of expression, family, and honor. These rights are granted to all human beings by virtue of their being human.

On the level of constitutional rights, however, the universalistic school allows diversity and accepts differences between Muslims and non-Muslims. These differences manifest themselves in the debates about interreligious marriage, inheritance, and giving testimony against a suspect from another religion. In addition, non-Muslims are not required to join the army or serve the state; these may be seen as advantages or restrictions. Yet there is one clear restriction: a non-Muslim cannot be the leader of a Muslim state. Non-Muslims can occupy any position other than the top leadership.

The Communalist School

Not all Muslim jurists in the classical period agreed with the views of the universalistic school. The competing communalist discourse, represented by Muhammad ibn Idris al-Shâfii[19] (d. 820), Malik Ibn Anas[20] (d. 795), and Ahmad ibn Hanbal (d. 855), maintains that having dhimmah is a status that only Muslims can enjoy. Non-Muslims achieve that status by virtue of the compact they make with the Muslim authority. From this perspective, dhimmah is a gained right and privilege; it is also the basis of other rights to be gained by virtue of signing a treaty with the Muslim authority. Enjoying legal personhood requires fulfilling the conditions of the treaty. Otherwise, it will be lost. One of the conditions of keeping legal personhood is to pay the special poll tax, *jizya*, to the state.[21]

In contrast with the universalist school, the communalist school lacks the abstract concept of human qua human as a possessor of rights. Instead, it relies on the religiously defined categories, such as disbeliever (*kafir*) and believer (*mu'min*). Nor does it support the concept of birthrights or natural rights as the Hanafis do. For the communalist school, all rights are gained and granted by the law. As mentioned above, the right to inviolability is gained by virtue of faith (*iman*) or a treaty of security (*aman*). One is automatically considered a citizen of the Islamic state if one is a Muslim, and consequently his dhimmah is respected. The non-Muslim who makes a treaty with the Islamic state can also become a citizen and gain the right to dhimmah. Only then can he become accountable and inviolable. By the treaty of dhimmah, Muslims take non-Muslims under their protection, grant them minority rights, and accept accountability for their security. In other words, they take non-Muslims under their dhimmah.

JIZYA

From the perspective of the communalist school, the *jizya* is the fee for dhimmah, which entitles one to inviolability, *'ismah,* and residence in the Muslim state, *sukna.* But universalist jurists argue otherwise. For them, dhimmah and 'ismah are not subject to monetary exchange; they are inalienable universal rights that are granted at birth.[22] From this perspective, as Muslims are required to pay *zakat* and other annual charities and taxes, non-Muslims are also required to pay taxes in the form of jizya. For the Hanafi school, jizya is acceptable from all non-Muslims, including the People of the Book and non-Arab pagans, the only exceptions being Arab pagans and polytheists. For the Shafi'i school, jizya is acceptable only from the People of the Book and Zoroastrians and not from the followers of other religions because the Qur'an and *hadith* did not list them among those who are allowed to make peace with Muslims and pay jizya.[23] Mughals and Ottomans, who followed the Hanafi school, indiscriminately collected the jizya from the followers of all religions.

Among non-Muslim subjects, only the able, the young, the healthy, and working male adults were required to pay jizya. Non-Muslim women, children, the aged, the sick, the unemployed poor, the disabled, and clergy were not required to pay jizya.

The jizya was negotiable if a territory surrendered willingly to Muslim rule and made a peace treaty with Muslims. Once the jizya was set for a certain amount after mutual agreement, the state was never allowed to change it unilaterally. If a territory was conquered by force, however, the amount of jizya, according to the Shafi'i school (one *dirham,* silver money, per month), was the same for all non-Muslim citizens regardless of their income level. By contrast, the Hanafis divided non-Muslims into three categories and required them to pay different amounts: a rich dhimmi was required to pay 48 dirham per year, a middle-class dhimmi was required to pay 24 dirham per year, while a low-income dhimmi was required to pay only 12 dirhams per year. It was possible to pay the tax in monthly installments.

If a dhimmi accepted Islam, according to the Hanafi school, his past jizya charges were waived. The Shafi'i school, however, required that past jizya be paid because this was debt in exchange for a good, namely, the security that the dhimmi received.[24]

In the Ottoman Empire, jizya traditionally was collected by the representatives of each millet organization to be transferred in whole to the state. The income generated by these taxes was used to sponsor public services. During the nineteenth century, the Ottomans standardized taxation for all citizens, Muslims and non-Muslims, and abolished jizya.

BASIC RIGHTS IN ISLAM

Regardless of the above noted debate about how rights are justified, Islamic law grants six basic rights to individuals, be they Muslims or non-Muslims. An individual is presumed to be part of a millet organization. Nevertheless, individuals have rights that are granted to them universally and equally regardless of their religion, race, gender, and culture.

These rights are seen as given and are not subject to debate. Therefore, they are termed "axiomatic principles of law" (al-daruriyyat al-shar'iyya). They are also known as "the objectives of law" (maqasid al-shari'ah). These rights are

1. the right to the inviolability of life ('ismah al-nafs or 'ismah al-dam);

2. the right to the inviolability of property ('ismah al-mal);

3. the right to the inviolability of religion ('ismah al-din);

4. the right to the inviolability of freedom of expression ('ismah al-'aql);

5. the right to the inviolability of family ('ismah al-nasl); and

6. the right to the inviolability of honor ('ismah al-'ird).

Because these rights are universally granted, minorities also enjoy them. Accordingly, the life, property, religion, mind, family, and honor of all individuals are inviolable, regardless of their inherent, inherited, and acquired qualities such as race, religion, gender, culture, and education.

Minorities are allowed to fully practice their cannon law provided that they do not contradict these six axiomatic principles of Islamic law. In that case they are prevented from practicing those rules that explicitly violate these basic rights. Consequently, Muslim rulers prohibited the practice of *sati* in India.[25] Likewise, they prohibited the practice of marriage with siblings among some Zoroastrians in Iran.

Communal Rights of Minorities in Islamic law

Broadly speaking, Islamic law recognizes two major groups: Muslim millet and non-Muslim millet, each with subdivisions. The Muslim millet is divided into two major groups—Shiites and Sunnis—again each with subdivisions, each of which is called *madhhab* (referring to a school of law). The subgroups under the non-Muslim millet are also called millet. The institutional organization in which all these groups are connected to each other horizontally and to the Muslim ruler vertically is called the millet system.

This pluralistic social and legal structure was facilitated by a particular view of "normative truth." The pluralistic theological approach to legal and moral norms made possible the coexistence of different millets and madhhabs side by side within a given society. Islamic jurisprudence accepted from the very beginning that normative truth is multiple rather than unique. There was a consensus that this was the case at the societal level. The disagreement was on whether normative truth was multiple in God's eye as well: Does God allow human beings to have different normative rules while He knows that only one of those rules is correct? Or does He perceive all of the normative rules adopted by human beings as correct? Are all these "valid" opinions and doctrines as long as they are supported by rational and scriptural evidence, even though they might not be "correct" in God's eye? The answer to this question can never be known or judged. Even those who accepted the view that the normative truth is one in God's eye agreed that He allowed it to be diverse in human society and therefore He is not going to punish those who failed to know the truth in His eye. Prophet Muhammad said: "God gives two rewards to a legal scholar who is correct in his reasoning and judgment (*ijtihad*) while He gives one reward if the legal scholar is mistaken in his reasoning and judgment after doing his best." What counts here is the serious and sincere effort to discover what is right and wrong given the limitations of the human mind. In any case, Muslim jurists in the classical era assumed that God allowed normative truth to be multiple at the societal level.

Muslim jurists also accepted that Muslims are not the only representatives of normative truth. Secular and religious reasoning would lead human beings to the normative truth whether it is carried out by Muslims or non-Muslims. Human beings have the intellectual capacity to discover what is right and wrong in all matters, said the Mu'tazilites.[26] For them the role of divine revelation is only to affirm what human beings can discover rationally by using their minds. Yet the majority of the jurists from the Sunni and Shiite schools agreed that even if we cannot discover what is right and wrong by relying solely on our minds, our minds concur with what is right and wrong after we learn it from divine books and prophets.

Furthermore, Islamic law grants "validity" to pre-Islamic religions, which legitimizes the practice of their law by minorities. Muslim theologians accepted that all divine or heavenly religions are from God and that their followers worship the same God. Religion with God is one, yet it is revealed to all nations with their languages because God never punishes a society without sending them a messenger who speaks their language. From this perspective, all religions are previous forms of God's religion, which preserved their authentic form to varying degrees. Islam came to affirm the message of these earlier religions and to correct what was tampered with, but not to falsify them. From this approach, the superiority of Islam is in being the most recent message of God to humanity:

> Those who believe (in the Qur'an), and those who follow the Jewish (scriptures), and the Christians and the Sabians,—any who believe in Allah and the Last Day, and work righteousness, shall have their reward with their Lord; on them shall be no fear, nor shall they grieve (The Qur'an, *Al-Baqarah* 2:62).

Based on this view toward other religions, Muslim jurists agreed that the laws of previous religions may also serve as a source of Islamic law in case there is a problem for which Muslim scriptures do not provide an answer. This principle is commonly known as "laws of the ones before us" (*shar' man qablana*). It may be seen as going beyond merely allowing the non-Muslim canonical laws to exist or tolerating their practice by their followers, as it also opens a gate for give and take, for dialogue and constructive interaction. From this perspective, the truth is shared by all social groups and not monopolized by a particular group or the ruling class. The multiplex understanding of the normative truth from a relationalist, as opposed to essentialist, perspective helped reduce social and cultural tensions among divergent truth claims. It also prevented differences in values, beliefs, and ideas from turning into social and political conflicts.[27]

Muslim Minorities

The current literature on minorities under Muslim rule focuses exclusively on the non-Muslim minorities and millet system without exploring the Muslim approach to the multiplexity and multiplicity of normative truth, which is the Islamic approach to non-Muslim minorities and the millet system. Yet, if one wants to have a full picture, one has to pay attention to Muslim minorities as well.

What was life like for minority Muslims—those who were ethnically, linguistically, or denominationally different from the majority? Muslim minorities were primarily organized as madhhabs and Sufi orders, two enduring forms of civil association in Muslim societies. The relationship between Arabs and non-Arabs was problematic during the rule of the Umayyads (c. 661–750 CE) because of their official ideology based on Arab supremacy, *shu'ubiyyah*. During the rule of the Abbasids, there was a period of religious persecution known as *mihna*, when the state adopted the view of one madhhab, namely the Mu'tazilah, and oppressed the others. There were also periods when Sufis were persecuted because of their belief in *wahdat al-wujud*, the best example of which is the life and execution of Hallaj.[28]

These are some of the rare examples that demonstrate what could have happened if Islamic law had not been objectively implemented. Overall, however, during Islamic history, Muslim minorities, be they ethnic or religious, enjoyed complete equality with the Muslim majority. It is possible to say that the problems mentioned above were instigated for nonreligious reasons, such as political motives, clash of interests, and personal rivalries.

Classical Islamic law required that non-Muslim communities be organized as millets under their religious leader and follow their canonical law. As explained above, the Islamic view of other religions and legal systems plays a large role in justifying such legal pluralism. In the Qur'anic verse cited, the mention of Sabians, who are not part of the People of the Book, may be seen as an indication that religious freedom is not restricted only to the People of the Book. The status of millet and the rights emanating from it are granted not only to Christian and Jewish communities—who are considered People of the Book, *Ahl al-Kitab*—but also to Zoroastrians in Iran and to Hindus and Buddhists in India.[29]

Consequently, throughout Islamic history a great number of Muslim and non-Muslim communities managed to maintain their identity and culture.[30] This does not mean that there were no discriminatory practices toward non-Muslims, particularly when viewed from the perspective of modern human rights standards. However, compared to the practices of their counterparts during the Middle Ages, the degree of religious freedom granted by Islamic leaders, although it looks insufficient today, was immensely progressive and crucial.

Structurally speaking, classical Islamic law granted non-Muslim communities the right to considerable autonomy or self-determination in their internal affairs regarding education, tax collection, law, and religion, along with exemption from military and state service. When needed, the leaders of the millets negotiated the amount of jizya with the state. They also established and managed their own institutions such as places of worship, schools, courts, and pious foundations.

Andalusia is usually seen as the prime example of the embodiment of tolerance in Islamic law pertaining to minorities. Yet Andalusia is not an exception but, rather, an extension of Islamic practice in other parts of the world. For instance, the roots of the millet system may be traced back to the Medina document, or *Al-Wathiqa*, signed by the leaders of the religious communities at the time of the Prophet Muhammad.[31] The four Rightly Guided Caliphs who came after Muhammad, as well as the Umayyads, Abbasids, and the Mughals, also contributed to the evolution of the system. Therefore it would be a mistake to think that the millet system is an Ottoman innovation.

THE CASE OF THE OTTOMAN EMPIRE

The Ottoman Empire followed the tradition of the millet system,[32] and, beginning with Sultan Mehmet Fatih (the Conqueror), improved its institutional structure by explicitly stating that rights of non-Muslim communities be addressed to them in the royal decrees. These decrees were called *Ahdnâme*, and because they were accompanied by the Sultan's pledge, they had the force of an international contract.

Greek Orthodox Christians were not established as the first millet after the conquest of Constantinople by Sultan Mehmet, as is commonly assumed in the literature. Rather, they had the same communal rights all along under the Seljuqs and the Ottomans prior to the conquest of Constantinople in 1453. The Orthodox patriarch had been granted the same rights as the leaders of other communities that had previously come under Islamic rule .The patriarch was allowed to apply Orthodox law in secular and religious matters. What Sultan Mehmet, who after the fall of Constantinople considered himself the Eastern Roman Emperor, did was to grant a charter to the patriarch of the Orthodox Church, Genady II.

As the policy of religious pluralism and multiculturalism was consolidated by the millet system, it allowed the Jews to form their own community and to establish independent religious, educational, and legal institutions in Istanbul. Historians commonly note that the freedom that was granted to the minorities within the Ottoman territories attracted large numbers of displaced Jewish communities that were among the victims of persecution in Spain, Poland, Austria, and Bohemia:

> [W]hile in Russia, Rumania, and most of the Balkan states, Jewish communities suffered from constant persecution (pogroms, anti-Jewish laws, and other vexations), Jews established on Turkish territory enjoyed an altogether remarkable atmosphere of tolerance and justice.[33]

Armenians were another religious community that formed a millet under the Ottoman rule. Sultan Mehmet issued a royal decree, or Ahdnâme, establishing the Armenian patriarchy in Istanbul under Patriarch Hovakim. As a result, a great number of Armenians reportedly emigrated to Istanbul from Iran, the Caucasus, eastern and central Anatolia, the Balkans, and Crimea—not because of persecution or forced dislocation but because Sultan Mehmet made his empire a true center of Armenian life. The Armenian community thus expanded and prospered together with the Ottoman Empire until the Armenian uprising after the collapse of the millet system.

In 1463, Sultan Mehmet also granted a charter of rights, or Ahdnâme, to the Bosnian Franciscans. The Ahdnâme granted significant rights to the Catholic Church in Bosnia represented by the Bosnian

Franciscan official Andjeo [Angel] Zvizdic. Andjeo Zvizdic "Vrh-
bosanski" remained the "Sultan's faithfull subject, obedient to his rule,"
as he had promised in the Ahdnâme, until his death in 1498. The Ahdnâme stated the following:

> I, Sultan Muhammad Khan, announce to all the people that the re-
> cipients of this imperial firman, the Bosnian Clergy, are held by me
> in my great esteem, and I therefore order that: No one should dis-
> turb or meddle with them or their churches. They are to live in
> peace in my Empire. Those who have fled should feel free and se-
> cure. They should return and settle again without fear in their mon-
> asteries. They must not be disturbed either by My High Majesty, or
> by my viziers, employees, subjects or any other inhabitants of my
> Empire. No one should attack, insult or endanger either them, or
> their lives, or property, or their churches. And if they wish to bring
> some person from foreign lands into my state, they are allowed to
> do so. Having made this imperial order, I make the following sacred
> pledge: By the Creator of earth and heavens, who feeds all his crea-
> tures, by the seven sacred books, by our great Prophet, and by the
> sword which I wear, I swear that no one shall act against what has
> been written here while this clergy remains subject to my service
> and faithful to my rule (Dated, May 28,1463).

These decrees should be seen as a confirmation of existing rights
rather than the granting of new rights that had not existed in Islamic
law. In fact, issuing such decrees has been a custom of Muslim con-
querors. For instance, it is commonly known that Caliph Umar issued
decrees with a similar content to the Christians after Jerusalem came
under Islamic rule in 637 CE.

The millet system may be seen as a major reason why the Ottoman
Empire survived so long. The system afforded the right of self-gover-
nance to the communities and delegated power and the numerous administrative burdens to local authorities. Representatives of the
millets, but not Ottoman officials, had to deal with their communities
on many issues. The religious heads of these communities were elected
by the members of their communities, and their role was to establish
and maintain relations with the state. These leaders served as the
bridge between the government and their communities, thus func-
tioning as intermediaries between the state and society. The different

community groups themselves acted independently of the state, as they had the authority to organize their own judicial, educational, and religious affairs.[34]

MANAGING INTER-MILLET RELATIONS

Regulating the relations among different millets was a daunting task and posed some problems. One issue was the testimony of a witness against a suspect of another religion. Some Muslim jurists ruled out such testimony because of possible prejudice due to the religious difference between suspect and witness; some jurists, however, thought that religious difference was not an issue in testimony. Another problematic issue was that of interreligious marriage. Muslim males were allowed to marry women of the People of the Book, but Muslim women could not. This was based on the rationale that a Muslim man would respect his wife's faith because, as a Muslim, he is required to believe in her prophet and sacred book. But a Christian or Jewish man does not believe in the Prophet Muhammad and the Qur'an and consequently is not obliged by his religion to respect a Muslim woman's faith. Non-Muslim communities, too, completely restricted interreligious marriage.

Apostasy and blasphemy were among the most common crimes according to all canonical laws during the Middle Ages, including Islamic law. Yet the punishment classical *Shari'a* stipulated for an apostate was never implemented unless the case was politically charged. Building new worship places required permission from the state. Ottomans did not proselytize non-Muslims, nor did they allow followers of other religions to proselytize each other.

Members of different millets were required to carry symbols of their faith in public places to reveal their identity. This regulation regenerated the existing configuration of authority relations within the society by maintaining social identities. It was also part of freedom of expression. However, during the period of modernization, as the role of religion in forming social identities declined and secular identities prevailed over religious identities, such rules looked obsolete and restrictive.[35]

The most important restriction in the millet system, from a modern perspective, was not allowing a non-Muslim to take the responsibility of "general leadership," or *al-walaya al-'ammah*. Under classical Islamic law, non-Muslims were allowed to serve as minister and prime minister (*vizier*), but not as the ruler of the state. The same restriction applied—and in many Muslim countries still applies—to Muslim women as well, because according to classical Islamic law only a Muslim man can assume the responsibility of "general leadership."

MODERNIZATION: FROM *DHIMMI* TO CITIZEN AND FROM MILLET SYSTEM TO NATION-STATE

As the Muslim states, notably the Ottoman Empire, gradually began to modernize, the definition of minority shifted from religious to ethnic terms as a secular approach to identity gained prevalence.[36] "Minority," under classical Islamic rule, meant primarily non-Muslim citizens. Their entitlement to human and constitutional rights had been a major issue in classical Islamic law as discussed earlier. But after the abolition of the millet system, religious differences lost all consequence, and, instead, ethnic differences became important.[37] The millet system had minimized the impact of ethnic differences. But over the course of the nineteenth century, especially after the collapse of the religion-based millet system, such differences became important. This trend was accompanied by the rise of a nationalist spirit, which during the nineteenth century spread from Europe to the Muslim world. Consequently, ethnic groups became conscious of their identity and began to demand more rights, if not total independence. In response, the Ottomans had to reform their traditional system and grant equal citizenship and rights to their non-Muslim subjects.

The Ottoman Reforms

The first royal decree—the Royal Decree of the Rose Garden (*Gulhane Hatt-i Humayunu*)—was launched in 1839 during the *Tanzimat* Reforms.[38] This declaration, which may be seen as the first declaration of human rights by a Muslim state, assured all citizens of their basic rights, namely the right to life, property, freedom of religion, protection of honor, education, employment, and due process. The Tanzimat declaration was grounded on the doctrine of *'ismah* (inviolability) in Islamic law. The document is especially significant for its recognition of equal rights for Christians in education and in government administration. Exemplifying egalitarian principles, the decree declared: "All Muslim or non-Muslim subjects shall benefit from these rights. Everyone's life, chastity, honor, and property is under the guarantee of the state according to the Shari'a laws." Representatives of all religious groups and the ambassadors of European states were present at the declaration ceremony, which ended with a prayer led by the *Shaikhulislam* (the highest-ranking Muslim cleric and administrator of religious affairs on behalf of the sultan).

The second stage in this process of reform was the meeting of the Royal Advisory Council of the Ottoman Sultan (*Meclis-i Meshveret*, advisory assembly) on March 24, 1855, to discuss how to reform the rights of minorities, particularly the Christians, in the empire—rights that had been regulated for centuries in accordance with classical Islamic law. The reformist sultans and statesmen aspired to make the Ottoman state a modern European nation. These aspirations, coupled with internal pressures from minorities and international pressures from European allies and foes, triggered reform in Islamic law. Following their deliberations, the advisory council sought the opinion and blessing of the Shaikhulislam for their decisions and obtained it. On March 26, 1855, the council met once again and produced the most important official document on reforms regarding minority rights in Islamic law.

The document advised the Ottoman sultan to adopt modern European standards on the following six issues: accepting the testimony of non-Muslims as equal to that of Muslims; granting non-Muslims high-level official titles; employing them in state jobs; accepting them into military service; allowing them to restore their churches; and abolishing jizya. The document stated that these reforms would facilitate the membership of the empire in the European community of states, as recommended by Lord Palmerston, the British ambassador in Istanbul. Sultan Abdulmejid (who ruled 1839–1861), approved the document.[39]

The Islamic justification for these reforms came from the work of Muhammad Shaibani, the great student of the Muslim jurist Abu Hanifa (699–765), *Kitab al-Siyar al-Kabir*.[40] Through this work, the Ottoman scholars and statesmen who were attempting to reform the law according to the universalistic perspective rediscovered the roots of the universalistic school in Islamic law. This strategy proved useful for getting the *ulema*—community of legal scholars—and the Muslim community to comply with the new reforms.

Thus the ground was laid to treat non-Muslims as equal citizens with Muslims under Islamic law with the blessing of the caliph and Shaikhulislam, the highest authorities of Islamic faith. This process of reform heralded the beginning of the end of a period during which non-Muslims had been treated differently. On February 18, 1856, these reforms were announced to the world in the form of a human rights declaration (*Islahat Fermani*). In 1875, the Imperial Edict on Justice (*Ferman-i Adalet*) provided for the independence of the judicial courts and ensured the safety of judges. Eventually, in 1876, these reforms found their way into the first Ottoman constitution, which clearly stated that all citizens of the state are equal.

The 1876 Constitution marks the most important step along the road to the rule of law in the Ottoman Empire, initiating the First Constitutional Period (which continued for one year under the rule of Abdulhamid II). Although this first constitution is seen as somewhat restrictive regarding the exercise of powers, it nevertheless for the first time recognized a parliamentary system. The constitution had provisions covering basic rights and privileges and the independence of courts and the safety of judges, among other aspects. In 1908, the Young Turks who dethroned Abdulhamid II launched the Second Constitutional Period and laid the foundations of a parliamentary system, which continued until the fall of the Ottoman State.[41]

Constitutionalism and the End of the Millet System

Proclamation of the constitutional system meant the abolishment of the traditional millet system and the introduction of the modern nation-state model to the Ottoman Empire.[42] As the dhimmis became equal citizens on the individual level, there was no need for them to continue to form separate communities under their religious leaders based on their religious and cultural identity. Rather, the identity of major millets such as the Jewish, Armenian, Rum, Catholic, and Orthodox became subsumed under a new identity, namely that of the Ottoman millet. The concept of millet (religious community) shifted from religious to secular and ethnic content and came to mean "nation." But this project of integrating all religious communities under one national identity failed, however, as ethnic groups rose as minorities with distinct secular identities. The Ottomans were caught unprepared about how to cope with this new wave of secular nationalism, as Islamic law was silent on this new configuration of relations based on ethnic identity. [43]

The transition from a religious approach in the network of social relations to a secular ethnic approach was not easy. Armenians may be seen as the victims of the collapse of the millet system under which, as did all other religious minorities, they led a safe and secure life with their Muslim neighbors for centuries. As secular ethnic identity gained prominence, the role of secular leaders increased. Most of these secular leaders worked to secure independence from the Ottoman Empire in the Balkans and Anatolia. With the collapse of the empire, scores of nation-states emerged on its territory with religious and secular regimes.

The emergence of nation-states turned ethnic groups into minorities as the newly founded nation-states adopted national identities. In the modern era, the Muslim Brotherhood has opposed the demands of ethnic minorities who have been deprived of their cultural rights, rights that they enjoyed under classical Islamic rule. This opposition has been justified mostly in the name of national cohesion.

The foregoing shows that both secular and religious approaches may be used to promote or undermine minority rights. Muslim countries with secular regimes as well as those with religious regimes provide ample examples for this observation. Today, both religious and secular regimes in the Muslim world are frequently accused of violating the rights of minorities—evidence that the type of regime is not the determining variable in this process.

Outside observers who are not familiar with the Islamic world's cultural dynamics might mistakenly attribute the restrictive practices of secular regimes in Muslim countries to Islamic law. In reality, however, the secularization of the legal system in the Muslim world indicates a complete departure from the principles of Islamic law as outlined here. Turkey is a prime example of a Muslim country with a secular legal system where minority rights are highly restricted.

Secularization of the Turkish legal system did not automatically solve problems of minority rights. Some problems were solved but new problems emerged. The Kurds did not pose a problem under Ottoman rule, as they were allowed to use their language and maintain their culture. Yet they felt disturbed by the new nationalist ideology and the restrictions imposed on the practice of their culture and language. Religious minorities, too, experienced problems that they had not experienced under Ottoman rule, in particular problems concerning religious education due to the state monopoly on religious education. Even Muslims have experienced problems in religious education for the same reason. The Turkish Republic nationalized pious foundations and outlawed Sufi orders. Missionary activities by Christians were also prohibited. And finally, the headscarf, which a considerable number of Turkish Muslim women wear, was banned during the 1980s for students and state employees. Similarly, around the same time, male students, professors, and state employees were banned from having a beard.

On the other hand, after the collapse of the Ottoman Empire, some of the newly established states like Saudi Arabia professed to practice Islamic law. Some others, including Pakistan, Sudan, Iran, Afghanistan, and Nigeria, recently joined them by declaring Shari'a rule because of the public pressures during the last decades of the twentieth century. Yet their interpretation and practice of Islamic law pertaining to minorities has not been as tolerant as that of the Ottomans or other traditional Islamic states. In particular, the implementation of the penal law of Islam has gone beyond reasonable limits and has drawn protests from both Muslims and non-Muslims. None of these states has adopted the universalistic Islamic tradition outlined here. Instead, they have chosen to implement the most restrictive interpretations of Islamic law.

CONCLUSION

The views in Islamic law regarding minority rights have been heterogeneous and open to evolution, as demonstrated by the reforms in the late Ottoman Empire, the most recent large Muslim state with a multiethnic and multireligious population. The universalistic school in Islamic law can be used to build upon to make Islamic law compatible with contemporary understanding of minority rights.

From this perspective, the Ottomans had already solved many of the problems that Muslims intellectuals are struggling with today. However, the chain of memory was broken after the collapse of the Ottoman

Empire, as the reform movement in Islamic law was discontinued and the reformist Ottoman legacy was forgotten. Consequently, today Muslim intellectuals must struggle with the same questions that Ottoman intellectuals and rulers dealt with almost two centuries ago. The classical Shari'a perspective regarding minority rights posed problems in several areas, such as testimony, jizya, and service in the state and the military, and Ottoman scholars had reformed the rules of Shari'a in those areas in the first part of the nineteenth century. Unfortunately, their efforts are completely forgotten today by the specialists in Islamic law who are trying to configure a solution to these problems.

The Ottoman state set an early example for how to deal with minorities under Islamic rule from a liberal perspective. The Ottomans as a world power acted pragmatically in legal matters and thus allowed the evolution of classical Shari'a as required by global developments. Muslim states in the present world should learn from the Ottoman experience and advance it further. This requires restoring the broken chain of memory and reclaiming the Ottoman reformist legacy.

Today, once again, *adamiyyah* (humanity) must be revived as the foundation of human rights for both Muslims and non-Muslims. It provides a solid conceptual ground to build upon. Yet, as discussed earlier, even this school discriminated against minorities at the level of *hajiyyat* (requirements) and *tahsiniyyat* (improvements). These practices, which look discriminatory today from the perspective of modern human rights, should be removed by making *adamiyyah* the foundation of all rights at all levels, namely at the level of universal human rights and domestic constitutional rights.

Today, as a result of emigration from the Muslim world, millions of Muslims are living in the West and, therefore, Muslims have an additional reason to treat minorities as equal citizens under Islamic law.

Another reason to treat all citizens and human beings equally under Islamic law is the fact that globalization has made the entire world a small village. But neighborly relations in this village have yet to be established. Educating Muslims to treat non-Muslims as their equals by reviving the universalistic school of Islam in respect to rights and assuring the world that Islamic law will treat non-Muslims equally are two major steps in this direction. Reciprocity is a universal legal and moral principle that we, as humanity, should adopt today on the individual and communal level. The traditional wisdom, "Do unto others as you would have others do unto you" and "Say not, I will do so to him as he hath done to me,"[44] is more valid today than ever before.

Notes

[1] See Robert Devereux, *The First Ottoman Constitutional Period* (Baltimore, Md.: Johns Hopkins University Press, 1963).

[2] Although the concept of "secularism" was included in the Constitution of the Republic of Turkey in 1937, the principle of secularism had existed de facto since the foundation of the republic. With the abolition of the Caliphate and the Ministry of Shari'a (Islamic Law) and Foundations on March 3, 1924, during the Republican period, and by providing for the unification of education and later the unification of the judiciary, significant steps were taken on the course to secularism. These steps were followed by others such as the Hat Reform, closure of the Sects and Convents, changing the weekly holiday from Friday to Sunday, and the adoption of the Latin alphabet and the Gregorian calendar. Finally, with an amendment put into practice with Law No. 3115 dated February 5, 1937, "secularism" became a constitutional principle.

[3] As historians of religion commonly state, Islam is an Abrahamic religion like Judaism and Christianity. All three religions emerged in the Middle East and extended westward. Islamic law facilitated give-and-take with other legal traditions, as Islamic jurisprudence considered pre-Islamic legal traditions (*shar' man qablana*), mainly Jewish and Christian canon law, as one of the sources of Islamic law. Therefore, it initially built upon the legacy of the previous legal traditions, but later evolved to such an extent that it began to influence Jewish and Christian canon laws.

[4] In Arabic, *al-Ijtihad la yanqud bi al-ijtihad.* In other words, "an *ijtihad* does not nullify another *ijtihad.*" From this inclusive perspective, whether an *ijtihad* is followed by the majority or the minority makes no difference to the validity of the legal opinion and doctrine.

[5] On this discussion, see Ibn al-Qayyim al-Jawziyya, *Ahkam Ahl al-Dhimmah,* ed. Subhi Salih (Beirut: Dar al-'Ilm li al-Malayin [1961], 1983), 3–18. Accepting *jizya* (poll tax) is an indication of granting the status of *dhimmah* to non-Muslims. Ibn al-Qayyim, a Hanbali scholar, writes: "The doctors of law disagreed about from whom *jizya* is collected. This is after they agreed that it is collected from People of the Book and the Zoroastrians. Abu Hanifa said: It is collected from People of the Book, the Zoroastrians and the non-Arab pagans. It is not accepted from Arab pagans. Ahmad ibn Hanbal also supported that view in a narration from him" (p. 3). He also defends the view

that all people, pagans as well as People of the Book , should be granted *dhimmah* because it is in their best interest to get a chance for direct exposure to Islam and the benefits it affords to humanity. Allah loves this more than killing them (p. 18). See also Ibn Abidin, *Hashiya Ibn 'Abidin Radd al-Mukhtar 'ala Durr al-Mukhtar*, vol. 12, ed. Husam al-Din b. Muhammad Salih Farfur (Damascus: Dar al-Thaqafa wa al-Turath, 2000/1421), 726–728; Burhanaddin 'Ali ibn Abi Bakr al-Marghinani (d. 593/1197), *al-Hidayah Sharh Bidayah al-Mubtadi*, vol. 2, ed. Muhammad Muhammad Tamir and Hafiz 'Ashur Hafiz (Cairo: Dar al-Salam, 2000/1420), 861–862.

[6] See Sri Ram Sharma, *The Religious Policy of the Mughal Emperors* (Bombay: Asia Publishing House, 1972); Zulfaqar Mubed (d. approx. 1670 AD), *Hinduism During the Mughal India of the 17th Century*, trans. David Shea and Anthony Troyer (Patna: Khuda Bakhsh Oriental Public Library [1843], 1993).

[7] Only in the modern era did voices emerge to abolish all schools in Islam and unite them under one official viewpoint, a failed attempt by Muslim modernists such as Rashid Rida from Egypt. His call was very appealing to Turkish modernists who wanted to standardize Islamic faith and practice. For the Turkish translation of Rashid Rida's work, see Muhammed Reşid Riza (1935/1354), *Mezahibin Telfiki ve Islam'in Bir Noktaya Cem'i*, trans. Ahmed Hamdi Akseki (Istanbul: Matbaa-i Amidi, 1914). Paradoxically, with this project Muslim modernists advocated suppressing divergent discourse communities in the Islamic community, instead of promoting more diversity in discussions concerning the understanding and practice of religion.

[8] When Napoleon Bonaparte tried to stir revolt among the Armenian Catholics of Syria and Palestine to support his invasion of 1798–1799, his ambassador in Istanbul replied: "The Armenians are so content with their lives here that a revolt is impossible." Turkish tolerance towards non-Muslims was so well known that many famous historians commented on their virtue. Voltaire said: "The great Turk is governing in peace twenty nations from different religions. Turks have taught the Christians how to be moderate in peace and gentle in victory." Philip Marshall Brown stated: "Despite the great victory they won, Turks have generously granted to the people in the conquered regions the right to administer themselves according to their own rules and traditions." Likewise, J. W. Arnold stated: "It is an undeniable historical fact that the Turkish armies have never interfered with the religious and cultural affairs in the areas they conquered." Even Politis, who was the foreign minister in the Greek government led by Prime Minister Venizelos, said: "The rights and interests of the Greeks in Turkiye could not be better protected by any other power but the Turks." See http://www.atmg.org/ArmenianProblem.html.

[9] Benjamin Braude and Bernard Lewis, eds., *Christians and Jews in the Ottoman Empire* (New York: Holmes-Meier Publishers, 1982); Bernard Lewis, *The Jews of Islam* (Princeton, N.J.: Princeton University Press, 1987); by the same author, *Race and Slavery in the Middle East: An Historical Inquiry* (New York: Oxford University Press, 1990); Bat Yeor, *The Dhimmi: Jews and Christians under Islam*, trans. Paul Fenton, David Maisel, and David Littman (Rutherford, N.J.: Farleigh Dickinson University Press, 1985); again by the same author, *The Decline of Eastern Christianity under Islam: From Jihad to Dhimmitude Seventh–Twentieth Century*, trans. Miriam Kochan and David Littman (London: Associated University Press, 1996).

[10] See the works of Michael Perry, in particular his recent book, *Under God? Religious Faith and Liberal Democracy* (New York: Cambridge University Press, 2003). On the relationship between religion, morality, and law, contrast the works of H. L. A. Hart (*The Concept of Law*, 2nd ed. [Oxford: Oxford University Press, 1997]) and his American critics such as Lon Fuller (*Morality of Law* [New Haven, Conn.: Yale University Press, 1964]) and R. M. Dworkin (*Law's Empire* [Cambridge, Mass.: Harvard University Press, 1986]). The recent edition of Hart's *The Concept of Law* has a postscript (pp. 238–276) where he responds to the critiques leveled by Fuller and Dworkin. Also see Harold Berman, *Faith and Law: The Reconciliation of Law and Religion* (Atlanta, Ga.: Scholars Press, 1993); by the same author, *Law and Revolution: The Formation of Western Legal Tradition* (Cambridge, Mass.: Harvard University Press, 1983); John Witte Jr. and Johan D. van der Vyver, eds., *Religious Human Rights in Global Perspective*, vols. 1–2 (Boston: Martinus Nijhoff Publishers 1996); Abdullahi A. An-Na'im, Jerald D. Gort, Henry Jansen, and Hendrik M. Vroom, eds., *Human Rights and Religious Values: An Uneasy Relationship?* (Grand Rapids, Mich.: William B. Eerdman's, 1995; Robert Audi and Nicholas Wolterstorff, *Religion in the Public Square: The Place of Religious Convictions in Political Debate* (Lanham, Md.: Rowman and Littlefield, 1997); Christopher Eberle, *Religious Convictions in Liberal Politics* (New York: Cambridge University Press, 2002); Jeffrey Stout, *Democracy and Tradition* (Princeton, N.J.: Princeton University Press, 2004).

[11] The Turkish spelling is "millet." On the concept, see Recep Senturk, "millet," *TDV Islam Ansiklopedisi* [Turkish Encyclopedia of Islam], vol. 29 (Istanbul: Center for Islamic Studies [ISAM], 2003).

[12] For a detailed discussion of the philosophical and historical roots of this division in the classical Islamic law, see Recep Senturk, "*Adamiyyah* and *'Ismah*: The Contested Relationship between Humanity and Human Rights in Classical Islamic Law," *Turkish Journal of Islamic Studies*, no 8 (2002).

[13] In Arabic: *al-'Ismah bi al-Adamiyyah*. See, for example, al-Marghinani, *al-Hidayah Sharh Bidayah al-Mubtadi*, 852 and 865.

[14] In Arabic: *al-'Ismah bi al-iman aw bi al-aman*.

[15] For the meaning of *dhimmah*, see Ibn al-Qayyim, *Ahkam Ahl al-Dhimmah*, vol. 2, p. 475; Namr Muhammad al-Khalil al-Namr, *Ahl al-Dhimmah wa al-Walaya al-'Ammah fi al-Fiqh al-Islamic* (Amman, Jordan: al-Mektebet al-Islamiyya 1409/1988), 73–74.

[16] Al-Marghinani, *al-Hidayah Sharh Bidayah al-Mubtadi*, 471, 474.

[17] Sarakhsi, *Usul:* "*Li anna Allah ta'ala lemma khalaqa al-insan li haml amanatih akramahu bi al-'aql wa al-dhimmah li yakuna biha ahlan li wujub huquqillah ta'alah alayhi. Thumma athbata lahu al-'ismah wa al-hurriyyah wa al-malikiyyah li yabqa fa yatamakkana min ada'i ma hummila min al-amanati. Thumma hazihi al-amanah wa al-hurriyyah wa al-malikiyyah thabitah li al-mar'i min hinin yuladu, al-mumayyiz wa ghayr al-mumayyiz fihi sawaun. Fakazalika al-dhimmah al-saliha li wujub al-huquq fiha thabit lahu min hinin yulad yastawi fihi al-mumayyiz wa ghayr al-mumayyiz.*"

[18] These rights may also be compared with the second and third generation of human rights (see chap. 2 in this volume).

[19] For an English translation of the views of Iman Shafi'i on jurisprudence, see Muhammad ibn Idris al-Shafi'i, *Al-Imam Muhammad ibn Idris al- Shafi'i's al- Risala fi Usul al-Fiqh: Treatise on the Foundations of Islamic jurisprudence*, trans. Majid Khadduri (Cambridge, England: Islamic Texts Society, 1987).

[20] For an English translation of the views of Iman Malik on law, see Imam Malik Ibn Anas, *Al-Muwatta: The First Formulation of Islamic Law*, trans. Aisha Abdurrahman Bewley (London: Kegan Paul International, 1989).

[21] The *jizya* tax is based on the following verse from the Qur'an: "Fight those who believe not in Allah nor the Last Day, nor hold that forbidden which hath been forbidden by Allah and His Messenger, nor acknowledge the religion of Truth, (even if they are) of the People of the Book, until they pay the Jizya with willing submission, and feel themselves subdued" (*Al-Tawbah* 9:29).

[22] On this discussion, see Ibn Qayyim al-Jawziyya, *Ahkam Ahl al-Dhimmah*, ed. Subhi Salih (Beirut: Dar al-'Ilm li al-Malayin [1961], 1983), 18–25. Ibn Qayyim refutes the Shafi'i view. See also al-Marghinani, *al-Hidayah Sharh Bidayah al-Mubtadi*, 865.

[23] See the Qur'an, *Al-Tawbah* 9:29. Bukhari, *Sahih*, "Kitab al-Jizya" (297/6); Malik, *al-Muwatta*, "Jizyat Ahl al-Kitab" (121/1). It is narrated that the Prophet Muhammad took *jizya* from the Zoroastrians of Bahrain; Umar took it

from the Zoroastrians of Iran and Uthman took it from the Zoroastrians of Barbar. See al-Marghinani, *al-Hidayah Sharh Bidayah al-Mubtadi*, 861. 'Umar bin Dinar narrated the following: "I was sitting with Jabir bin Zaid and 'Amr bin Aus, and Bjalla was narrating to them in 70 A.H. the year when Musab bin Az-Zubair was the leader of the pilgrims of Basra. We were sitting at the steps of Zam-zam well and Bajala said, "I was the clerk of Juz bin Muawiya, Al-Ahnaf's paternal uncle. A letter came from 'Umar bin Al-Khattab one year before his death; and it was read: "Cancel every marriage contracted among the Magians between relatives of close kinship (marriages that are regarded illegal in Islam: a relative of this sort being called *Dhu-Mahram*.)" 'Umar did not take the *jizya* from the Magian infidels till 'Abdur-Rahman bin 'Auf testified that Messenger of God had taken the *jizya* from the Magians of Hajar."

[24] Ibn Qayyim also accepts the Hanafi view and refutes the Shafi'i opinion, See Ibn Qayyim, *Ahkam Ahl al-Dhimmah*, 57. For the detailed regulations on *jizya*, see al-Marghinani, *al-Hidayah Sharh Bidayah al-Mubtadi*, 860–866; Abdullah b. Mahmud b. Mawdud b. Mawsili, *al-Ikhtiyar li al-Ta'lil al-Mukhtar* (Istanbul: Mektebet Pamuk, n.d.), 662–871; Ibn Abidin, *Hashiya Ibn 'Abidin Radd al-Mukhtar 'ala Durr al-Mukhtar*, 719–742; Ibn Qayyim, *Ahkam Ahl al-Dhimmah*, 22–100.

[25] The Mogul rulers of India outlawed the *sati* practice although they could not completely exterminate it. See Sri Ram Sharma, *The Religious Policy of the Mughal Emperor* (Bombay: Asia Publishing House, 1972), 42-44; Zulfaqar Mubed, *Hinduism During the Mughal India of the 17th Century*, 77.

[26] Richard C. Martin, Mark R. Woodward, and Dwi S. Atjama, *Defenders of Reason in Islam: Mu'tazilism from Medieval School to Modern Symbol* (Oxford: Oneworld, 1997); George Fadlo Hourani, *Reason and Tradition in Islamic Ethics* (Cambridge: Cambridge University Press, 1985).

[27] For the social implications of multiplexity of discourse on political culture, see Recep Senturk, "Towards an Open Science: Learning from the Ottoman Humanities," *New Millennium Perspectives on the Humanities*, ed. Judi Upton-Ward (New York: Global Humanities Press, 2002), 55–75; also by the same author, "Toward an Open Science and Society: Multiplex Relations in Language, Religion and Society," *Turkish Journal of Islamic Studies*, no. 5 (2001).

[28] The well-known Sufi Mansur al-Hallaj (857–922 CE) was condemned to death by the religious authorities in Baghdad for his unrestrained ecstatic utterances. See Louis Massignon, *The Passion of Al-Hallaj: Mystic and Martyr of Islam*, 4 vols., trans. Herbert Mason (Princeton, N.J.: Princeton University Press, 1982).

[29] For a detailed review of the arguments and counterarguments exchanged between universalistic and communalistic schools on whether dhimmah should be granted to the followers of religions other than Christianity, Judaism, and Zoroastrianism by allowing them to make peace with Muslims and pay , see Ibn Qayyim, *Ahkam Ahl al-Dhimmah*, 1–17; Namr Muhammad al-Khalil al-Namr, *Ahl al-Dhimmah wa al-Walaya al-'Ammah fi al-Fiqh al-Islamic*, 75–94.

[30] Braude and Lewis, *Christians and Jews in the Ottoman Empire*.

[31] See Mohamed Berween, "Al-Wathiqa: The First Islamic State Constitution," *Journal of Muslim Minority Affairs* 23, no. 1 (April 2003): 103–119. An article in this document states the following: "To the Jews who follow us belong help and equality. They shall not be wronged nor shall their enemies be aided. The Jews should contribute to the cost of war so long as they are fighting alongside believers. The Jews of the Bani Awf are one community with the Believers (the Jews have their religion and the Muslims have theirs), their freedom and their persons, except for those who behave unjustly and sinfully, for they hurt but themselves and their families."

[32] For a recent study on the millet system and the references cited there, see Macit Kenanoglu, *Osmanli Millet Sistem: Mit ve Gerçek* (Istanbul: Klasik, 2004). See also, S. J. Shaw, *History of the Ottoman Empire and Modern Turkey* (Cambridge: Cambridge University Press, 1977); by the same author, *Jews of the Ottoman Empire and the Turkish Republic* (New York: New York University Press, 1991); Halil Inalıck and Donald Quataert, eds., *An Economic and Social History of the Ottoman Empire: 1600–1914* (Cambridge : Cambridge University Press, 1997).

[33] P. Dumont, "Jewish Communities in Turkey during the Last Decades of the Nineteenth Century in the Light of the Archives of the Alliance Israelite Universelle," in Braude and Lewis, *Christians and Jews in the Ottoman Empire*, 209–242.

[34] See Ilber Ortaylı, "Osmanlı Imparatorlugunda Millet," *Tanzimat'tan Cumhuriyet'e Türkiye Ansiklopedisi*, vol. 4 (Istanbul: Iletişim Yayınları, 1985), 996–1001; see also, in the same volume, Cevdet Küçük, "Osmanlılarda 'Millet Sistemi' ve Tanzimat," 1007–1024.

[35] Paradoxically, during the last two decades Turkish authorities made the opposite mandatory by prohibiting the carrying and wearing of religious symbols in the public sphere. Later, France also adopted a similar approach.

[36] Muhittin Ataman, "Islamic Perspective on Ethnicity and Nationalism: Diversity or Uniformity?" *Journal of Muslim Minority Affairs* 23, no. 1 (April 2003): 89–120.

[37] P. Dumont., "Jewish Communities in Turkey during the Last Decades of the Nineteenth Century," 209–242; K. H. Karpat., "Millets and Nationality: The Roots of the Incongruity of Nation and State in the Post-Ottoman Era," in Braude and Lewis, *Christians and Jews in the Ottoman Empire*, 141–170.

[38] The term *Tanzimat*, which literally means "reorganization," refers to a period of modernizing reforms instituted under the Ottoman State from 1839 to 1876. In 1839, under the rule of Sultan Abdulmecid, the edict entitled Hatti-i Sharif of Gulhane laid out the fundamental principles of Tanzimat reform. Foremost among the laws was the security of honor, life, and property for all Ottoman subjects, regardless of race or religion. Other reforms, which sought to reduce theological dominance, included the lifting of monopolies, fairer taxation, secularized schools, a changed judicial system, and new rules regarding military service. Tanzimat ended in 1876 under Abdulhamid II's reign, when the ideas for a Turkish constitution and parliament were first implemented for a brief period before they were abolished by the same sultan. The constitution and parliament were reintroduced after Abdulhamid II was dethroned by the Young Turks in 1908.

[39] Mehmet Yıldız, "1856 Islahat Fermanina Giden Yolda Mes‚ruiyet Arayışıarı: Uluslararası Baskılar ve Cizye Sorununa Bulunan Çözümün Islami Temelleri," *Türk Kültürü Incelemeleri Dergisi* 7 (Istanbul 2002): 75–117.

[40] Abu Abdullah Muhammad ibn Hasan ibn Farqad al-Hanafi al-Shaibani, *Kitab al-Siyar al-Kabir* (The Detailed Book of Siyar), published with a commentary by Abu Bakr Shams al-Aimma Muhammad ibn Ahmad ibn Sahl al-Sarakhsi (d. 483/1090), *Sarh Siyar al-Kabir*, trans. Salahaddin Munajjid (Cairo: Jamiah al-Duwal al-Arabiyya, 1971). For an early Turkish translation see *Tercüme-i şerh-i siyeri'l-kebir*, trans. Mehmed Münib Ayıntabi (Istanbul: Matbaa-i Amire, 1825). For the English translation see *The Islamic Law of Nations: Shaybani's siyar*, trans. Majid Khaduri (Baltimore, Md.: Johns Hopkins University Press, 1966). For a French translation see *Le grand livre de la conduite de l'etat: Siyerü'l-kebir*, trans. Muhammed Hamidullah (Ankara: Türkiye Diyanet Vakfi, 1989).

[41] For the intellectual and political history of this period, consult, Serif Mardin, *The Genesis of Young Ottoman Thought* (Princeton, N.J.: Princeton University Press, 1962); M. Şükrü Hanioglu, *The Young Turks in Opposition* (New York: Oxford University Press, 1995).

[42] For a collection of Ottoman and Turkish constitutions, see Suna Kili and A. Şeref Gözübüyük, *Türk Anayasa Metinleri* (Ankara: Türkiye Iş Bankası, 1985).

[43] For a recent study on the nineteenth-century Ottoman reforms, see Ali Akyıldız, *Osmanlı Bürokrasisi ve Modernleşme* (Istanbul: Iletişim Yayınları, 2004).

[44] The Old Testament, Proverbs 24:29. This principle is the common core of universalistic thought in various legal systems, religions, and moral philosophies. Matthew's account reads: "Therefore all things, whatsoever ye would that men should do to you, do ye even so to them" (Matthew 7:12). Luke 6:31 closely resembles Matthew's words: "and as ye would that men should do to you, do ye also to them likewise."

CHAPTER SIX

THE CAUSES OF MUSLIM COUNTRIES' POOR RECORD OF HUMAN RIGHTS

Saad Eddin Ibrahim

Countries that have poor human rights records are frequently the same countries that have poor records in other aspects of economic, social, and political development. This assertion applies equally to Muslim and non-Muslim countries. Many scholars and political observers who question the compatibility of Islamic and democratic values argue that the essentialist and communalistic nature of Islam leaves no place in Muslim societies for individual rights, including basic political and civil rights.[1] However, a closer look at the realities on the ground demonstrates that the record of human rights in Muslim and Arab countries is not as poor as it is often assumed to be. Rather, the record is mixed. In fact, when these countries are measured along the United Nations development indicators, their record correlates very well with their rank on the United Nations Development Program's Human Development Index. Thus, countries that are performing poorly on that index also have very poor human rights records. The Freedom House index shows a similar correlation, as does the Transparency International index.[2] These correlations apply to all developing countries, including Arab and Muslim ones. In other words, a country's human rights condition reflects the state of its general economic, political, and social development.

Much of the history of the evolution of human rights in the West is not that different from what is currently happening in the Muslim world. Some may have forgotten a century-long debate among the U.S. founding fathers over the definition of who is a complete human being worthy of any rights at all. Or that it took another century entailing a civil war before slavery and its aftermath were eradicated in the United

States. Equal rights for women are still being contested. Some Western women, such as the Swiss, obtained their voting rights after their counterparts in several Muslim countries, such as Egypt, Turkey, and Tunisia.

Having questioned the assertion that Islam and human rights are incompatible, the fact remains that the human rights record of many countries with Muslim majorities leaves much to be desired. My competing hypothesis is that the state of human rights is mainly a function, not of religion, but of a country's overall level of socioeconomic development. How else could we account for the marked variations in respect to human rights among countries sharing the same religion, namely Islam?

After having established that the human rights record of Arab and Muslim countries is not inferior to that of other developing countries, one can concentrate on identifying the reasons behind the Arab and Muslim worlds' mediocre record on human rights, a situation that creates a divide between them and the West and causes tensions in their relations.

REASONS FOR THE HUMAN RIGHTS DIVIDE

Three factors explain the existing limitations with respect to human rights in Arab and Muslim countries. The first factor is the differences between despotic and non-despotic regimes. The second is the difference between textualists and contextualists. And, finally, the third is the very troubling challenge for democracy activists and civil society advocates whose message gets entangled in the process of resistance to Western hegemonic policies in the developing world.

Despotic versus Non-despotic Regimes

In recent years several countries in the Muslim world have undergone democratic transitions. Even within the Arab world, countries such as Morocco, Qatar, and Jordan have taken cautious but steady steps on the road to political liberalization and democracy. Other regimes, such as those of Tunisia, Libya, Syria, and Egypt, have grown more despotic in recent years in order to remain in power. In the 1950s and 1960s these regimes maintained a social contract based on the withholding of political and civil liberties in return for the provision of basic services, employment, and social justice. Today these regimes are no longer capable of fulfilling their part of the social contract and yet are not willing to democratize and share power. Thus civil and political rights and liberties are severely repressed, and these despotic regimes utilize both legal and extralegal means to maintain their power.

Textualists versus Contextualists

For Muslims, the Holy Qur'an is the divinely revealed book containing the words and commandments of Allah (God Almighty). Some Muslims take this sacred text literally to live by, and hence are referred to as "textualists." Others take the spirit, the broad guidelines, laid down in the Qur'an and adapt them to different and changing conditions in Muslim communities, and hence are referred to as "contextualists."[3] The outcome of this debate between the textualists and the contextualists will determine the direction for the future state of human rights in Muslim countries and, consequently, the future of political development of their respective communities.

In answer to the question of who speaks for Islam or for Muslims or what is typically an Islamic perspective on any issue, I would argue that what makes any matter Islamic is rooted in the text. I would further argue that in order to be defined as Islamic, a notion must be rooted in the two essential texts of Sunni Islam: the Qur'an and the tradition as enunciated by the Prophet Muhammad and later by his successors. A return to these fundamentals renders a notion, a theory, a perspective that is Islamic. What makes the above-mentioned concepts Muslim—not Islamic—is not the text; rather, it is the context. A multitude of parties have utilized Islam as a religion to justify their ideological leanings or political aims. While these parties might claim that their actions or beliefs are grounded in Islamic notions, I would argue that they are not based on Islam as a religion but, rather, depend on an array of social, political, and economic conditions pertinent to the specific Muslim context. A prime example of textualist Islam and Muslims is the Wahhabi movement of the eighteenth century in Saudi Arabia, of which Osama bin Laden and other followers consider themselves the legitimate heirs and who thus are contesting similar claims by the Saudi royal family. In contrast to the Wahhabis, most Muslims elsewhere in the world, from Indonesia to Morocco, either willfully or de facto subscribe to a variety of contextualist interpretations of Islam.

In sum, there are two perspectives on what is Islamic. One is based on the text and the other on the context. The text is always present—rigid, changing very slowly or never changing—whereas the context is constantly evolving.

This difference between text and context poses a dilemma not only for the relations between Muslims and non-Muslims or between the Islamic world and the West, notably the United States, but also for Muslims themselves. It creates a divide between the textualists and the contextualists, and between them and the secularists who are opposed to both. The debate between the textualists and the contextualists has a long history in the Muslim world. Great nineteenth-century Islamic reformers such as Muhammad Abduh and Jamal ed Din al Afghani focused on the importance of interpreting Islam in accordance with the logic of the temporal and spatial contexts. In recent years, the Muslim world has been placed between an immense extremist, and at times militant, Islamic current and the rigidity and inflexibility of the official religious establishment (such as the Al Azhar University in Egypt). Yet a few promising signs have appeared on the horizon, such as rare calls by Islamic scholars to reopen the door to *ijtihad,* or interpretation of the religion drawn directly from its sources. These calls resonate throughout the Muslim world.

U.S. Foreign Policy and Democratization Efforts in the Arab and Muslim World

Certain aspects of U.S. policy toward the Arab and Muslim world make the task of those working for democracy and human rights difficult, because they are perceived to be propagating a Western agenda at a time when there are many misgivings about the United States and its political aims in the Muslim world. The first problematic aspect is the double standard applied to Arab and Muslim countries; the second is the United States' one-sided support for Israel; and the third is U.S. unilateralism. In so many hotspots in the Arab world, such as Iraq and Palestine, the United States has acted alone without the collaboration of European powers, especially those that have positive images in the Arab world. This phenomenon has deepened Arab misgivings regarding U.S. unilateralism.

In my own work for the advancement of democracy and human rights in the Arab world, I have experienced the adverse consequences of these misgivings firsthand. As a result of these suspicions, human rights and democracy activists like myself are often accused of carrying out a Western agenda. Ironically, autocratic regimes that are allies of the United States cynically use this argument to discredit activists. The violation of human rights of other political activists, including Islamists, by various governments also has a deleterious effect on the advancement of democracy and human rights. Again, my own experience supports this contention.

As an academic, my work on Islamic extremists has spanned some 30 years. This association has given me three perspectives on these extremists. My first encounter was during my early work, when I conducted some of my fieldwork in a prison. Later, some 15 years after my initial research, I revisited them as a human rights defender. And, finally, 10 years later, I joined them as a fellow inmate as a prisoner of conscience.

When I returned to prison as a fellow prisoner, I found many of the extremists whom I had seen during my work 25 years earlier still in jail, a human rights abuse that should have been investigated as some had completed their sentences and the government of Egypt, a close ally of the United States, had refused to release them. This disregard of the rule of law was justified by the argument that as Islamists they continued to be potentially dangerous terrorists.

Ambivalence in American foreign policy vis-à-vis the Arab and Muslim world persists at a deep level. While the official U.S. foreign policy and discourses toward Arab and Muslim countries call for the promotion of democracy and better governance, the United States, through its financial support and trade relations, continues to collaborate with and maintain in power a multitude of corrupt and despotic regimes, including those in Egypt, Saudi Arabia, and even that of Saddam Hussein's Iraq during the Iran-Iraq War.

The United States has intervened militarily in Latin America 20 times in 100 years and 10 times in the Middle East during the last 50 years. Seventy-five percent of the world's refugees are Muslims. Unfortunately, most American citizens are unaware of these facts.

Moreover, not a single intervention has been on behalf of democracy. The most recent intervention, in Iraq, was supposed to usher in democracy not only there but also in the rest of the Arab world. But the chaos that has followed has obscured this democratic message. Rather, it has made that message one more example of the American double standard. No matter how intrinsically benign it may be, the message is often dismissed because of the suspect messenger.

THE IMPACT OF SEPTEMBER 11

The events of September 11, 2001, had a tremendous impact on the thinking of the Islamists in prison and my dialogue with them. Interestingly, after my release from prison in 2003, Islamists outside prison requested that we continue the dialogue that had started in prison.

An important part of the dialogue concerned the following dilemma: "Why has the world made so much fuss about you and said nothing about us?" This was a legitimate question to which, as I explained to them, I did not have an answer, because I was in prison with no access to those who demonstrated their support for me. However, I added, I could guess why the world was reacting more strongly to my incarceration. The reason I gave them was that, rightly or wrongly, activists around the word see me as someone sharing the same core universal values that human rights defenders around the world cherish. Furthermore, I was a human rights defender myself, which led to my imprisonment. By contrast, largely due to common misconceptions and the influence of the media, most Western activists view Islamists as opposing human rights by calling for the establishment of a social, religious, and political system that is inherently exclusionary to minorities and discriminatory to women and non-Muslims. Moreover, on some occasions, Islamists in the past have rejected non-Muslim human rights defenders struggling on their behalf.

In response, Islamists with whom I engaged in dialogue told me that they too believed in most of these values. I responded by saying, "If you believe in these values, you have failed to communicate your conviction to the world outside," and I advised them to do so by writing and speaking out. The events of September 11 made these Islamists aware that their radical discourse had been partly responsible for that event by affecting the minds and thoughts of young people. As a result, they felt a special responsibility for that event and wrote a book about 9/11, disavowing and for the first time condemning their fellow Islamists' actions and revising most of their previous convictions and stated principles and practices.[4]

The Islamists were also very intrigued by democracy and my challenge to them to declare their commitment to democracy. Initially,
they had reservations about democracy and about how one could be a
good Muslim and a good democrat. My observation of Christian democrats was well received. And several European ambassadors who were
aware of this dialogue provided the Islamists in prison with literature
they had requested about Christian democrats and how their movement had evolved. This literature proved that abiding by a particular
religious doctrine can in principle be, and has in practice been, reconciled with democracy as a political system.

Among the literature they read in prison was the Vatican's shifting
stand on democracy. In 1838, Pope Gregory XVI issued an edict con-
sidering democracy a "sinful heresy." The edict was a reaction to the
excessive anti-church/anti-clerical policies of the French Revolution and
Jacobin-style secularism. In the following century, the Bolshevik revolution and the emergence of communism and other authoritarian ideologies came to be seen as more detrimental to organized religion than
democracy. If anything, in the long run the Catholic church and its adherents fared better under democratic systems. Thus, following the
trauma of World War II, Pope Pious XII issued a new edict in praise of
democracy.

THE IMPACT OF EVENTS IN DEMOCRATIC
MUSLIM COUNTRIES

A number of recent developments in some Muslim countries have also
had a positive impact on Islamists' thought regarding the issues of democracy and human rights. The most important was the Turkish election in November 2003, which brought to power a party with deep
Islamic roots and a leader who is an observant Muslim. That election
was preceded by parliamentary elections in Morocco in September
2002 that also saw the emergence of several winners with Islamic agen-
das. The outcomes of these elections made the Islamists realize that Islam and democracy are not incompatible and that they can accede to
power through democratic means. Disappointment with the Islamic
government in Iran has also contributed to some Islamists' rethinking
of their stance on democracy.

Consequently, after I was acquitted in March 2003, many of the Islamists that I had met in prison wanted to continue the dialogue in order to get in touch with Western diplomats and Western academic and intellectual colleagues. (Some Western governments, notably the United States, refused to engage in this dialogue out of fear of offending the Egyptian government.)

Another hopeful sign in terms of convincing Islamists that they can be both Muslims and democrats is the fact that two-thirds of the Muslims in the world today—in Indonesia, Bangladesh, Malaysia, Turkey, and India (whose population includes 150 million to 200 million Muslims)—are living under democratic governments. These are not Westminster-style democracies or ideal democracies. However, thus far, no ideal democracy exists anywhere.

The results of the World Values survey conducted by the University of Michigan in 2002 are also encouraging.[5] According to this survey in 15 Muslim majority countries, between 88 and 93 percent of those sampled declared their commitment to democratic values.

CONCLUSIONS AND SUGGESTIONS ON HOW TO ADDRESS THE CHALLENGES

Three main obstacles prevent the consolidation of a better human rights record in the Arab and Muslim world.

The first is erected by the discrepancy between the hegemon's discourses and policy in the region, which diminishes the credibility of the notions of democracy and human rights—and their promoters—because they are associated in the popular psyche with foreign and imported concepts.

The other two impediments to an amelioration of the human rights record are domestic. Reluctance on the part of governments to loosen their grip on power leads them to disregard human rights and resist all calls to democracy. Meanwhile, some Islamic opposition forces violate the rights of women and minorities and allow the principles of democracy to function only within predefined and accepted boundaries.

As outlined above, however, several openings exist, most notably the following, through which advocates of democracy and human rights can surmount these obstacles.

One way is by connecting enlightened Islamic thinkers. These thinkers have existed throughout the times, but they have been marginalized by governments and by textualist and extremist Muslims.

The other way is by helping democratic forces in a nuanced, subtle way with the tools available. These tools include aid, trade, technology, and investment. However, one needs to use these tools intelligently. One is not obliged to use force or to be overbearing when approaching autocratic regimes to help potential democratic forces such as women, young people, civil society, and human rights organizations. Western governments can indicate to these regimes that if they want aid, favorable trade agreements, and investment, they should engage in sustainable democratic reform.

To avoid instability, a workable timetable is needed in the shape of a roadmap of expected positive developments, with aid, trade, and investment conditioned to that schedule. These incentives worked after Helsinki 1975 in Europe, and they have the potential to work in the Arab and Muslim world.

The Conference on Security and Cooperation in Europe (CSCE) has produced marvelous results in Eastern Europe and in the former Soviet Union. A similar process can do the same for the Arab world. Similar measures already have had some effect in Morocco, Bahrain, and Jordan. Ironically, it is the modernizing monarchies that are performing better in the Arab world—Bahrain, Qatar, Oman, and Morocco—whereas Egypt, Saudi Arabia, and, of course, Syria are reluctant to change and democratize.

Lastly, it is important that Western governments demonstrate their commitment to democracy in the Arab and Muslim worlds and follow a consistent policy in this regard.

Notes

[1] Such scholars include, among others, Ernest Gellner. See Ernest Gellner, "Civil Society in Historical Context," *International Social Science Journal* 43, no. 3 (1991): 133.

[2] The 2004 Transparency International Corruption Perceptions Index, http://www.transparency.org/surveys/;http://transparency.org/pressreleases _archive/2004/2004.10.20.cpi.en.html.

[3] However, as explained by Khaled Abou El Fadl in chapter 3 in this volume, the adaptation of text to context does not always lead to a progressive interpretation.—Ed.

[4] The book has not been translated into English. The Arabic title is *Kutub al Muraga'at li al gama'a al islamiya* [Books Reconsidering Islamic Associations].

[5] World Values Surveys, available at http://www.worldvaluessurvey.org/statistics/index.html.

CHAPTER SEVEN

HUMAN RIGHTS AND U.S. FOREIGN POLICY

RECONCILING IDEALS AND INTERESTS

Robert A. Pastor

The war in Iraq opened a gap between the United States and much of the world. The United Nations Security Council did not accept the administration's argument that it should invade Iraq because of an imminent threat that Saddam Hussein would use weapons of mass destruction or share them with terrorist organizations. After the invasion and the failure to find such weapons, the Bush administration used a second rationale for the war: to promote democracy and human rights in Iraq. Not surprisingly, this deepened the skepticism that had greeted the administration's first reason for going to war. Because the United States was wrong about the weapons of mass destruction in Iraq, many thought that the administration was disingenuous about wanting to promote democracy and human rights there. The Iraq war also opened a gap between America's self-perception as a veritable "city upon a hill" and the world's perception of America as an expansionist and possibly imperial hegemon.

The second rationale for the war was articulated by President George W. Bush on November 6, 2003, as the United States began to encounter stiff resistance in Iraq. In a speech at the National Endowment for Democracy, President Bush asserted that the United States fought the war on behalf of democracy. More broadly, he insisted that the pursuit of democracy would henceforth shape his entire policy toward the Greater Middle East because past policies that had underplayed democracy had failed: "Sixty years of Western nations excusing and accommodating the lack of freedom in the Middle East did nothing to make us safe—because in the long run, stability cannot be purchased at the expense of liberty." He concluded that "the United States has adopted a new policy, a forward strategy of freedom in the Middle East....The advance of freedom is the calling of our time; it is the calling of our country. From the Fourteen Points to the Four Freedoms, to the Speech at Westminster, America has put our power at the service of principle."[1]

President Bush's statement was powerful and clear, but many in the Middle East and the rest of the Muslim world believed that actual U.S. policies contradicted this statement. For example, the United States supported General Pervez Musharraf in Pakistan despite the fact that he had come to power by overthrowing a democratic government. Many Arabs asked how such a statement could be reconciled with U.S. policy toward Palestine, which for years impeded any movement toward free elections for fear that Yasser Arafat might prevail in such a free election. Or how could such a statement be reconciled with the strong support the United States had given and continues to give to Egypt, despite its government's repressive policies and its fraudulent elections?

EXPLAINING THE GAP

How does one reconcile President Bush's statement supporting liberty over stability with U.S. policies that seem aimed to support stability over liberty? There are several alternative explanations. The most obvious is that the United States is hypocritical—that it offers statements of principle to disguise its narrow self-interest.

A second explanation is incompetence: the president is sincere but incapable of executing U.S. policy effectively. This may be true of some of the Bush administration's policies, but with regard to the issues of human rights and democracy, the gap between rhetoric and policy, as President Bush acknowledged above, has a much longer history.

A third explanation is the existence of deep divisions within the executive branch over policy. Three decades ago, Graham Allison demonstrated that individual actors pursuing their rational ends could collectively produce an irrational or a nonrational outcome.[2] This could be due to bureaucratic politics, organizational process, misperception, interbranch politics, or any division within the United States that requires a compromise that aims to satisfy different interests rather than to most effectively pursue a single strategy.

Still, a fourth explanation is that the United States has always sought to balance its ideals with its interests, and that policy has frequently been a compromise, which, by definition, never fully satisfies either advocates of interests or ideals.

To assess which of these explanations might be the most compelling, I will look to another region of the world—Latin America—where the United States has a much longer history of trying to reconcile its power with its principles.[3] An historical analysis of U.S. policy toward the region might shed light on contemporary dilemmas in the Middle East and the rest of the Muslim world.

LESSONS FROM LATIN AMERICA

The British historian Gordon Connell-Smith once wrote that the question as to whether the United States supports democracy in Latin America is "essentially an academic exercise remote from reality, since the United States traditionally has supported cooperative dictators until they have outlived their usefulness, and notwithstanding all the rhetoric suggesting otherwise has pressed for free elections only when these have served its particular policy objectives."[4] This statement of American hypocrisy could be applied to U.S. policy in the Middle East and elsewhere. Historically, there are many examples of such double standards in U.S. policy. Yet this explanation does not capture the sweep of American history or American policy.

Looking at the history of U.S. policy toward Latin America and starting with the first major statement, the Monroe Doctrine, in December 1823, one sees a merger of two very different strands that have continued to define the policy and the debate in the United States. Monroe aimed to prevent the recolonization of Latin America by Europe, but the Monroe Doctrine also placed that realistic goal in an ideological context.

One view was represented by Henry Clay, the Speaker of the House of Representatives. Clay argued that the United States should come to the defense of democracy everywhere—not just in Latin America, but also in Greece and Hungary. A different view was espoused by Secretary of State John Quincy Adams, who argued that the United States should be cautious about making such grandiose statements, as they would do little more than provoke European powers to threaten the

United States. He urged the president to concentrate on what he could realistically achieve.[5]

Monroe chose to incorporate both views. In his "doctrine of the two spheres," Monroe declared that the United States is better than and different from Europe—that America stands for principle. The other component was Adams' realist focus; the purpose of the declaration was to warn Europe not to recolonize Latin America. Since then, the United States has constantly struggled with the debate as to whether it should be realistic or idealistic in its approach to foreign policy.

THE END OF ISOLATIONISM

In the twentieth century, the United States came out of its isolationist envelope and began to intervene internationally. In the nearest region—the Caribbean Basin—the United States intervened militarily 20 times by 1920. These interventions were not to promote human rights and democracy. Rather, they were motivated by the fear that a foreign rival might gain a foothold in the region, from where they could endanger the largest new investment of the United States—the Panama Canal. Despite this realistic motive for intervention, the United States always secured its exit by promoting elections that would bestow some legitimacy on the leaders who won them. In some cases, the United States used its power to influence the outcome, but at other times, the United States accepted the electoral outcome even when it did not reflect its preference.

By and large, the United States was not overly preoccupied with the moral implications of its foreign policy, at least not until Woodrow Wilson became president. Wilson injected "liberty" into the mainstream of his foreign policy. He sympathized with the peasants who fought for liberty and justice in the Mexican Revolution, and although he sent the U.S. Navy and marines to intervene in Mexico twice, he viewed the intervention as furthering U.S. interests in constitutional order.

From that moment through contemporary struggles in the Middle East and elsewhere in the Muslim world, the United States has faced the awkward dilemma of choosing between, on the one hand, supporting the democratic process and, on the other, opposing candidates who were viewed as unfriendly to the United States or its values. In

Latin America, this choice was posed most sharply in Guatemala in 1954 and in Chile in 1970–1973, and in both cases the United States chose to undermine democracy by covertly intervening to oppose popular candidates of the Left.

Like Wilson, President Jimmy Carter broke with his predecessors by integrating the themes of human rights and democracy into the soul of his foreign policy. More importantly, he decided to apply this goal against the United States' conservative "friends" as well as its radical enemies. In the past and in the administration of Ronald Reagan, the United States would use its support for democracy selectively and usually as an instrument to contain Communism and put it on the defensive. Carter was the first U.S. president to withdraw aid and support from right-wing governments even when they supported U.S. foreign policy and faced leftist insurgencies. This was seen most clearly in the case of Nicaragua. The contrast between the Carter administration's policy and that of President Reagan's was also sharpest in this case. President Reagan embarked on a costly covert war to overthrow the Nicaraguan government and impede a genuine election in 1984.[6] In short, President Reagan reverted to old ways, which were to promote democracy but only against left-wing regimes.

TWIN PENDULUMS, TWIN DEBATES

As Latin America swung on a pendulum between democracy and dictatorship, every setback was interpreted by the United States as being due to Latin America's flaws, while Latin Americans attributed any setbacks to U.S. intervention. Each traded places when there was movement in a positive direction, with the United States attributing it to the effectiveness of its policy and Latin Americans insisting that democracy occurred for internal reasons and despite U.S. policy.

An analysis of these cases suggests that the problem of interpretation stemmed from the fact that there were two pendulums—not one. The pendulum in Latin America was between the forces of authoritarianism and those of democracy; and that struggle, by and large, was determined by the forces within a particular country, although the momentum in neighboring countries was not an inconsequential factor. A similar dynamic appears to be working in the Middle East and many parts of the Muslim world today.

The second pendulum reflected the debate among U.S. policymakers. This debate is a bit confusing to the rest of the world and also to many Americans. And the debate has evolved over time. In the beginning, as noted earlier, it was simply a debate between the realists, like John Quincy Adams, who argued that the United States ought to focus on its vital security interests and not look for symbolic fights over democracy that could leave the nation vulnerable to attack by the great powers and, on the other side, the idealists who saw America's influence as dependent in part on its being a model for the rest of the world. For the idealists, the betrayal of U.S. values might yield a short-term benefit, but it would be at the cost of America's standing and thus would compromise its security. In the case of Guatemala in 1954, for example, the realists argued that defeating the leftist regime of Jacobo Arbenz eliminated the threat of Communism. By contrast, the idealists believed that the overthrow of a democratically elected Arbenz strengthened authoritarianism in Latin America and sent a message to leftists that the United States would not accept their victory in a free election. Thus, the left concluded that their only path to power was by violent revolution, and that was the path they chose, to the detriment of U.S. interests.[7]

Historically, in the United States, the Republicans have been the main supporters of realism, and the Democrats, of idealism. But the debates within each party have been almost as important as those between them.

One side of the debate within the Democratic Party is represented by President Franklin D. Roosevelt, who believed that the United States should not intervene in Latin America even in the struggle between dictators and democrats because, in the long-term, foreign governments can learn democracy only by making their own mistakes. Thus, when faced with the prospect of Anastasio Somoza seizing power in the mid-1930s, Roosevelt refused to take any steps that would prevent him from doing so. Roosevelt wanted Nicaraguans to maintain their democracy, but he placed a higher value on the principle of nonintervention.[8] On the other side of the Democratic debate, Woodrow Wilson and Jimmy Carter believed that the United States should play a more direct role in supporting democrats abroad. Wilson was prepared to use force to promote that goal; Carter thought that force would be counterproductive in the pursuit of democracy. This is the essence of the debate among the Democrats. Democrats agree, however, that America's power derives in considerable part from its pursuit of its ideals and that U.S. power is best pursued in cooperation with U.S. allies and with respect for international law and institutions.

In contrast, the Republicans have been classic realists, believing that the United States should intervene abroad only if national security or economic interests are threatened. While Republicans have shared the same ideals as Democrats, they have believed, as John Quincy Adams did, that the United States should be careful not to overextend itself on behalf of moral crusades. So, for example, Republicans view Saudi Arabia as an ally, despite its authoritarian leaders, because of America's need for secure supplies of oil and because Islamic radicals are viewed as the most likely alternative to the Saudi royal family.

From World War I until the outbreak of World War II, the dominant debate within the Republican Party was between the isolationists, who believed that the United States should stay out of the world's conflicts, and the unilateralists, who believed that the United States should defend its interests by itself and not allow allies or international organizations to constrain U.S. policy. Except for a period of about five years before the United States' entry into World War II, the unilateralists largely won that debate. After World War II, the isolationists became a marginal and inconsequential force, and during much of the Cold War, Republican presidents were also multilateralists.

Since the election of George W. Bush, the debate within the Republican Party has taken a new turn. With the multilateralists in decline, the major debate is occurring between the classic realists, who do not want to rock the friendly authoritarian regimes, and the neoconservatives, who have pressed for a pro-democracy agenda. Thus far, President Bush's rhetoric shows the ideological influence of the neoconservatives, but his policies demonstrate the caution of the classic realists. That explains the gap between statements and policies.

It is not always easy to sort out the debate and the policy, but at its most basic, the United States is seeking the best way to pursue both interests and ideals. In crafting specific policies, leaders face difficult tradeoffs on questions related to national security, timing, and economics. For example, should one withhold aid from a poor country because its leader is abusing the human rights of its citizens when that aid could help its poor people? This is not an easy question, and the answers have not been consistent.

CHALLENGES OF THE POST–COLD WAR ERA: THE MIDDLE EAST AND THE MUSLIM WORLD

In the post–Cold War era, the United States has been faced with a similar challenge and essentially the same choice: Should the United States support the democratic process, regardless of the outcome, or should it only support democratic parties that are friendly to the United States? If supporting democracy means allowing Islamic parties to come to power by a free election, would that, in effect, mean "one man, one vote, one time"? If so, the United States might unintentionally help its enemies to overthrow friendly, although authoritarian, regimes and replace them with unfriendly, authoritarian regimes. This dilemma explains why the United States has given massive amounts of aid to President Hosni Mubarak of Egypt even though he imprisons human rights and pro-democracy activists like Saad Eddin Ibrahim who are only seeking free elections and respect for basic rights and the rule of law. This also explains why the United States and Europe supported the Algerian military when it shut down the electoral process in 1991 for fear that Islamists might win. That choice, as explained here, is a variation on an old theme.

The substantive debate as it relates to democracy in the Middle East and the rest of the Muslim world is whether free elections can yield democracy or just a new brand of anti-American authoritarianism. The essence of democracy, Robert Dahl reminds us, is institutional uncertainty.[9] The democratic process is a risky one, and a malevolent party or candidate could come to power, as Adolf Hitler did in 1933. But if one compares the number of times that an Adolf Hitler wins an election with the number of elections won by genuine democrats, then the overwhelming odds favor the democrats. The argument for democracy grows even stronger if one examines the cases when free elections were interrupted or undermined because of fears of the outcome. The interventions in Guatemala in 1954, Chile in 1973, and Algeria in 1991 led to tens of thousands of deaths and tragically polarized societies.

The lesson from these experiences is highly relevant to the Middle East and other parts of the Muslim world. If one tries to exclude or marginalize a group that enjoys some popular support in order to maintain security and democracy, one will achieve neither. The best way to assure both is to find a formula for inclusion, not exclusion.

Can Islamists be moderate democrats? The Turkish military answered that question negatively until Prime Minister Recep Tayyip Erdogan won the 2003 election, and they have found him to be remarkably Western, democratic, and moderate. This does not mean that all future Islamists would be democrats, but it also means that we should not assume that they will not.

CONCLUSION: THE WAY FORWARD TO DEMOCRACY

In the first decade of the twenty-first century, the central challenge for the United States in the Middle East and the rest of the Muslim world is how to facilitate movement toward human rights and democracy.

A set of principles is essential, but a single formula will be elusive. The policy needs to be adapted on a country-by-country basis. Here, the United States needs to rely on the advice of courageous democrats in each country.

For example, in the case of Egypt, one should begin to construct a policy on human rights and democracy by consulting with pro-democracy and human rights activists like Saad Eddin Ibrahim, who will have a much better sense as to how quickly and in what ways a policy would be most effective.

To be effective, the United States must be seen as committed to democracy. Today, however, the image of the United States in the Middle East and the Muslim world is poor. How does one enhance the credibility of the United States, and therefore its effectiveness over time in pursuing this long-term interest? Part of the answer to this question depends on whether the United States is perceived as supporting the democratic process or opposing a certain group of actors. If Islamists believe that the United States will never permit them to take power by elections, as the Left concluded in Latin America, then they have no incentive to pursue a peaceful democratic process, and the prospects of violence increases.

To advance democracy, the United States must create political space for all groups. It must also develop a process that can allow people who are angry or alienated to gain a stake in that process. It is also necessary to find ways to allow people to evolve. This takes time.

I base this conclusion partly on my experience in Nicaragua in various capacities over 35 years—as a student, as a member of the National Security Council under President Carter when we tried unsuccessfully to mediate a democratic transition, and, finally, as a director of a team from the Carter Center, a nongovernmental organization led by Jimmy Carter, which successfully mediated a democratic transition in 1990. In 1989, when the campaign for the presidency began, none of the leading political actors in Nicaragua could be considered "democratic." The two leading candidates—Sandinista president Daniel Ortega and the leader of the opposition, Violete Chamorro—had no experience in free elections or democracy or even in a process that required compromise. Nonetheless, through a deliberate and intensive mediation process orchestrated by former U.S. president Jimmy Carter, all evolved, and by the time of the elections, all had begun to accept the basic tenets of democracy.

My experience in the Middle East also has convinced me that people are capable of evolving if one gives them political space and takes them seriously. One such experience was in Palestine during the election of 1996 where I was helping to organize the international observation of those elections. After the assassination of Yehiya Ayyash, a Palestinian leader of Hamas who was accused by the Israelis of orchestrating suicide bombings, former president Carter sent me to meet with Hamas leaders. Carter was worried that Hamas would unleash a wave of violence that would make the elections impossible and would endanger his delegation. I spent two days with the Hamas leadership, during which time I tried to understand where they were coming from. This was very hard to do, as their organizations sent young people to explode themselves and murder innocent civilians. Nonetheless, the Hamas leaders were candid. In the end, they promised a ceasefire through the elections, and they kept that promise. They also promised retaliation two weeks after the elections, and unfortunately they kept that promise as well.

In the course of those talks I learned a lot about the Hamas leaders and their perspective, and I came to believe that the same process that succeeded in such an unlikely place as Nicaragua might also succeed in the Middle East. Much would depend on the United States—whether it would respect a dialogue with all parties, whether it could obtain the necessary credibility, and whether it would make the hard choice of accepting the process rather than rejecting some parties.

Europe and Latin America could contribute to this effort because for the last four decades Christian parties in those regions have groped for a path to incorporate democracy into their political philosophy. Similarly, many in Arab countries and other Muslim countries are struggling to find ways to reconcile Islam with democracy. Christian Democrats in Europe and Latin America could help.

Finally, the most important lesson to be drawn from the experience of democracy in the developing world and U.S. policy on democracy emerges from the definition of democracy: democracy is a framework to choose leaders. Democracy is not a panacea; it is nowhere close to perfect. It is simply a way to select and replace leaders and, by doing so, to keep them accountable to the people. It is also the best way to deal with minorities because it provides a path for minority representation. However, that path needs to be secured. The rights of minorities—whether based on ethnic or religious ties or political ideology—need to be secured in order for everyone to be secure.

The United States has much to contribute to the debate—provided it learns from history and trusts that democracy is, as Winston Churchill once said, the worst form of government except for "all those other forms that have been tried from time to time."[10]

Notes

[1] White House Press Secretary, "President Bush Discusses Freedom in Iraq and Middle East," remarks by President G. W. Bush at the twentieth anniversary of the National Endowment for Democracy, November 6, 2004, http://www.whitehouse.gov/news/releases/2003/11/20031106.2.html.

[2] Graham Allison, *Essence of Decision* (Boston: Little, Brown, 1971).

[3] For a study on how the United States tried to integrate these two factors in its policy toward the world during the Carter administration, see Zbigniew

Brzezinski, *Power and Principle: Memoirs of the National Security Adviser, 1977–1981* (New York: Farrar, Straus, and Giroux, 1983).

[4] See Gordon Connell-Smith's review of a book by John Martz in *Journal of Latin American Studies* 21 (October 1989): 618.

[5] For a survey of U.S. policy, see Robert A. Pastor, *Exiting the Whirlpool: U.S. Foreign Policy toward Latin America and the Caribbean* (Boulder, Colo.: Westview Press, 2001).

[6] See Robert A. Pastor, *Not Condemned to Repetition: The United States and Nicaragua*, rev. ed. (Boulder, Colo.: Westview Press, 2002).

[7] Many of the Sandinistas pointed to the case of U.S. efforts to overthrow the democratically elected government of Salvador Allende in Chile as the reason they pursued violent revolution in Nicaragua. Ibid.

[8] For a more extensive development of this debate, see chap. 11, "Promoting Democracy: Pushing on the Pendulum," in Pastor, *Exiting the Whirlpool.*

[9] See Robert A. Dahl, *Democracy and Its Critics* (New Haven: Yale University Press, 1989).

[10] Winston Churchill, House of Commons, November 11, 1947.

CHAPTER EIGHT

CONCLUSIONS

Shireen T. Hunter

Nearly six decades after the adoption of the Universal Declaration of Human Rights, and despite the passing of several other important human rights documents in the following decades, debate about fundamental aspects of human rights continues.

Three issues are the subject of particularly intense debate. These are the universality of the concept of human rights as embodied in the UDHR and other international documents; the shifting basis for defining what constitutes inalienable human rights and resolving the tension between secular conceptions of rights and religious beliefs; and the range and scope of applicability of human rights. As noted by Ann Elizabeth Mayer in chapter 2,

> Especially since the mid-1980s, claims have been made that international human rights law is imbued with values that are essentially Western and are incompatible with non-Western traditions. Official claims regarding how 'Asian values' or Islamic tradition may require distinctive approaches to human rights have been put forward as ways to challenge the ideal of human rights universality that was central to the original UN system.

Indeed, the Islamic world has been perhaps the most important arena for debate on the universality versus the relativity of the human rights concept and where the debate has been most intense. However, Muslim and Asian countries have not been the only ones to challenge the universality of international human rights legislation. As noted by Mayer, the United States, too, has chosen not to ratify a number of human rights conventions. Nevertheless, as clearly explained by Khaled

Abou El Fadl and Saad Eddin Ibrahim, the issue of Islamic particular-ism has too frequently been used by authoritarian secular govern-ments as well as conservative clerical establishments to deny the Muslim peoples and non-Muslim citizens of Islamic states their basic rights.

Yet, this debate on universalism-versus-particularism has had one important result. It has forced Muslim intellectuals, thinkers, and even ordinary people to delve into the question of human rights in Islam and try to identify to what extent current understanding of the Islamic vision of human rights is reflective of the fundamental and overreach-ing ethical values and injunctions of Islam, notably the sanctity of hu-man life and the paramount importance of justice and mercy in regulating all aspects of Muslims' lives. The result has been new and creative work in this field, of which the three chapters in this volume dealing with various aspects of human rights issues in Islam are excel-lent examples.

The authors of those chapters reach three basic conclusions. The first is that Islam contains within itself notions of rights, notably the principle of the sanctity of human life, and overreaching ethical values that, properly interpreted and codified, would lead to the development of a system of human rights largely compatible with the UDHR.

To illustrate, Recep Senturk, in discussing the question of minority rights in Islam demonstrated how the universalistic school of thought in Islam, as first formulated by Abu Hanifa, grounds human rights on the concept of humanity, *adamiyyah,* and advocates equal rights for all human beings regardless of their inherited and innate qualities such as class, race, color, language, religion, and ethnicity.

Similarly, Riffat Hassan argued that Qur'anic injunctions and the overreaching ethical principles of Islam, such as justice and mercy, properly interpreted, guarantee equal rights for women. She blames present-day problems facing Muslim women, and the unfavorable conditions of women in Muslim societies, on the patriarchal traditions of Muslim societies—many of which predate the advent of Islam.

A second conclusion: Sadly, as Khaled Abou El Fadl explains, from the twelfth century onward, Muslim jurists and thinkers have failed to create a body of laws and regulations built upon the essential rights recognized in Islam and the ethical principles underpinning them. Had they done so they would have given rise to an Islamic system of human rights closely resembling the UDHR. Instead, Muslim jurists and thinkers have tended to adopt a restrictive definition of these rights. Moreover, since the twelfth century they have tended to support existing laws rather than trying to challenge those laws that clearly run counter to the spirit of Islam's ethical values, such as justice and mercy, and the rights of people recognized in Islam. The result has been that, while Islam recognizes rights for Muslims—and, according to some schools, rights for all human beings—that if properly interpreted would be largely compatible with the UDHR, currently there is no coherent and elaborate system of human rights in Islam. The seeds of such a system clearly exist, however, and need only careful tending to bear fruit.

A third conclusion is that the mostly secular governments of most Muslim countries deny their citizens basic rights that in no way are in contradiction of Islamic injunctions, a practice that has further hindered the development of an Islamic system of human rights largely compatible with the UDHR.

This situation inevitably creates tensions between the Muslim world and the United States—and the West—and makes dialogue on the human rights issue more difficult. What is encouraging is the emergence of a growing number of Muslim scholars and thinkers, including, increasingly, female scholars, who are trying both to revive the earlier, more expansive interpretations of rights in Islam and to offer new interpretations by the application of such concepts as *ijtihad* (independent interpretation) and *maslahah* (public good). Their ultimate objective is to develop an Islamic system of human rights more in line with the principles enshrined in the UDHR and other international human rights conventions.

This intellectual trend and the scholars pursuing it still face serious resistance from existing repressive governments, clerical establishments, and other conservative elements in the Muslim world. Therefore, it will take considerable time before a significant body of new work is produced and enough people are mobilized to force a change in the existing laws to make them compatible with the basic rights recognized in Islam and, more importantly, with the ethical norms most valued by Islam, such as justice and mercy. Nevertheless, the emergence of this trend and the scholars pursuing it indicate that the Islamic world is awakening, albeit slowly, from its long intellectual slumber on matters related to human rights.

Another complicating factor in U.S. and Western relations with the Muslim world as they pertain to the issue of human rights is the continuing challenge of reconciling ideals and interests. This dilemma results in the selective application of human rights principles by the United States—and the West—to various Muslim countries, thus raising charges of a U.S. and Western double standard. Robert Pastor, in his chapter, discussed how this dilemma in the past, especially during the period of the Cold War, had complicated the United States' relations with Latin-American countries. Pastor points out that during the Cold War, the United States faced the dilemma of how it could or should go about promoting democracy in Latin America if democratization led to the victory of leftist forces. Today, America is facing a similar dilemma in regard to Islamist groups in the Muslim World, especially in the Middle East.

Saad Eddin Ibrahim also stressed the negative impact of the inconsistency in U.S. policy on human rights as it pertains to the Islamic world, especially the Middle East. He points out that the selective and sporadic application of human rights standards to the Muslim world undermines those activists, secular and Islamic, who are working to advance the cause of human rights.

The discussion and analysis in this volume also suggest certain guidelines for future actions by the United States—and the West—and Muslim countries and intellectuals, actions that are the most likely to help advance the cause of human rights, help develop an Islamic concept of human rights largely in line with the UDHR, and help bridge the gap between the United States and the Muslim world in respect to human rights.

The following are the most important of these guidelines:

First, all countries must show respect for human rights by their deeds and not simply by signing declarations and conventions with no serious intent of implementing them.

Second, all countries, notably the Muslim majority states, should adopt a holistic as opposed to selective approach toward human rights. Thus they should give equal weight to civil rights, political rights, social rights, and economic rights.

Third, cultural differences should not be used as an excuse to deny people their basic rights.

Fourth, Muslim majority countries should pay special attention to the case of women and take steps to eliminate discriminatory practices against them.

Fifth, Muslim majority countries should guarantee the rights of their religious minorities.

Sixth, reformist thinking in Islam should be encouraged, thus helping to develop an understanding of human rights in Islam that is compatible with the UDHR and, in the process, eliminates religious and cultural justifications for disregarding human rights. This is necessary because of the pivotal role of Islam in Muslim societies and because progressive ideas rooted in Islam stand a better chance of gaining acceptance among Muslims.

Seventh, the United States and the West should refrain from selective application of standards for human rights and should show a sustained commitment to human rights globally and in the Muslim world. Such an approach may entail short-term risks, but in the long term its benefits will outweigh the risks.

Preoccupation with the rights of human beings and the struggle to acquire and maintain those rights is as old as humanity itself. Progress toward the recognition of basic human rights has not been easy or uninterrupted. On the contrary, there have been serious lapses, including in the last few years. Even today, large segments of humanity are deprived of some or all of their basic human rights.

What *is* different today is that, with the communications revolution and globalization, questions related to human rights are no longer merely in the sovereign domain of states. Rather, they are of global concern. Moreover, disregard for human rights is becoming a source of regional and international instability, thus necessitating greater international dialogue and cooperation to prevent the violation of basic rights. U.S.–Muslim dialogue in this respect constitutes a significant component of the broader international cooperation necessary to secure respect for human rights.

SELECTED BIBLIOGRAPHY

Abou El Fadl, Khaled. *Speaking In God's Name*. Oxford: Oneworld Publications, 2001.

Al-Shafii, Muhammad ibn Idris. *Al-Imam Muhammad ibn Idris al-Shafi'i's al- Risala fi Usul al-Fiqh* [Treatise on the Foundations of Islamic Jurisprudence]. Translated by Majid Khadduri. Cambridge, England: Islamic Texts Society, 1987.

An-Na'im, Abdullahi A, Jerald D. Gort, Henry Jansen, and Hendrik M. Vroom, eds. *Human Rights and Religious Values: An Uneasy Relationship?* Grand Rapids, Mich.: William B. Eerdmans, 1995.

Berman, Harold. *Faith and Law: The Reconciliation of Law and Religion*. Atlanta, Ga.: Scholars Press, 1993.

Brzezinski, Zbigniew. *Power and Principle: Memoirs of the National Security Adviser, 1977–1981*. New York: Farrar, Straus, and Giroux, 1983.

Devereux, Robert. *The First Ottoman Constitutional Period*. Baltimore, Md.: Johns Hopkins University Press, 1963.

Donnelly, Jack. *Universal Human Rights in Theory and Practice*. Ithaca, N.Y.: Cornell University Press, 1989.

Falk, Richard. "A Half Century of Human Rights: Geopolitics and Values." In *The Future of International Human Rights*, edited by Burns H. Weston and Stephen P. Marks. Ardsley, N.Y.: Transnational Publishers, 1999.

Glendon, Mary Ann. "Foundations of Human Rights." *American Journal of Jurisprudence* 44 (1999): 1–14.

Hourani, George Fadlo. *Reason and Tradition in Islamic Ethics.* Cambridge: Cambridge University Press, 1985.

Hunter, Shireen T., and Huma Malik, eds. *Modernization, Democracy, and Islam.* Westport, Conn.: Praeger/CSIS, 2005.

Ishay, Micheline R. *The History of Human Rights: From Ancient Times to the Globalization Era.* Berkeley: University of California Press, 2004.

Ishaque, K. M. "Islamic Law: Its Ideals and Principles." In *The Challenge of Islam,* edited by A. Gauhar. London: Islamic Council of Europe, 1980.

Jullundhri, R. A. "Human Rights in Islam." In *Understanding Human Rights,* edited by A.D. Falconer. Dublin: Irish School of Ecumenics, 1980.

Lauren, Paul Gordon. *The Evolution of International Human Rights: Visions Seen.* Philadelphia: University of Pennsylvania Press, 1998.

Mardin, Serif. *The Genesis of Young Ottoman Thought.* Princeton, N.J.: Princeton University Press, 1962.

Martins, Richard C., and Mark R. Woodward, with Dwi S. Atmaja. *Defenders of Reason in Islam: Mutazilism from Medieval School to Modern Symbol.* Oxford: Oneworld Publications, 1997.

Mayer, Ann Elizabeth. *Islam and Human Rights: Tradition and Politics,* 3rd ed. Boulder, Colo.: Westview, 1999.

————. "Universal versus Islamic Human Rights: A Clash of Cultures or a Clash with a Construct?" *Michigan Journal of International Law* 15 (1994): 307–404.

Mernissi, Fatima. *The Veil and the Male Elite: A Feminist Interpretation of Women's Rights in Islam.* Translated by Mary Jo Lakeland. Reading, Mass.: Addison-Wesley, 1991.

Perry, Michael J. *The Idea of Human Rights: Four Inquiries.* New York: Oxford University Press, 1998.

Primus, Richard A. *The American Language of Rights.* New York: Cambridge University Press, 1999.

Senturk, Recep. "*Adamiyyah* and *'Ismah*: The Contested Relationship between Humanity and Human Rights in Classical Islamic Law." *Turkish Journal of Islamic Studies,* no 8, (2002).

Smith, Wilfred Cantwell. *Islam in Modern History.* Princeton, N.J.: Princeton University Press, 1957.

Waltz, Susan. "Universalizing Human Rights: The Role of Small States in the Construction of the Universal Declaration of Human Rights." *Human Rights Quarterly* 23 (2001): 44–72.

Weston, Burns H. "Human Rights." *New Encyclopedia Britannica*, 15th ed., vol. 20. Chicago: Encyclopedia Britannica, 2002.

Wronka, Joseph. *Human Rights and Social Policy in the 21st Century.* Lanham, Md.: University Press of America, 1998.

INDEX

Page numbers followed by the letter n *refer to end-of-chapter notes.*

ABOUT THE EDITORS AND CONTRIBUTORS

Khaled Abou El Fadl is professor of law at the UCLA School of Law. He also serves on the board of Human Rights Watch and was appointed by President George W. Bush to the Commission on International Religious Freedom. His most recent books include *Islam and the Challenge of Democracy* (Princeton University Press, 2004) and *The Place of Tolerance in Islam* (Beacon Press, 2003).

Riffat Hassan is professor of religious studies and humanities at the University of Louisville, Kentucky. She is the founder of the International Network for the Rights of Female Victims of Violence in Pakistan, and her publications include numerous writings on Muhammad Iqbal, women in Islam, Islam and interreligious dialogue, and human rights in Islam.

Shireen T. Hunter is the director of the Islam Program at CSIS. Her latest publications are *Modernization, Democracy, and Islam*, coeditor and contributor (Praeger, 2005), *Islam in Russia: The Politics of Identity and Security* (M. E. Sharpe, 2004), *Islam: Europe's Second Religion*, editor and contributor (Praeger, 2002), and *The Future of Islam and the West: Clash of Civilizations or Peaceful Coexistence?* (Praeger, 1998).

Saad Eddin Ibrahim is professor of political sociology at the American University in Cairo. He is the founder and the first secretary general of the Arab Human Rights Movement and the founder and chairman of the Ibn Khaldun Center for Development Studies, Cairo.

Huma Malik is the deputy director of the CSIS Islam Program. She is the coeditor of *Modernization, Democracy, and Islam* (Praeger, 2005) and *Integrating Muslim Communities in Europe and the United States* (CSIS, 2003).

Ann Elizabeth Mayer is associate professor of legal studies at the Wharton School at the University of Pennsylvania. Her recent publications include "Shifting Grounds for Challenging the Authority of International Human Rights Law: Religion as a Malleable and Politicized Pretext for Governmental Noncompliance with Human Rights" in *Human Rights with Modesty: The Problem of Universalism*, Andras Sajo, editor (Martinus Nijhoff, 2004).

Robert A. Pastor is director of the Center for Democracy and Election Management and professor of international relations at American University in Washington, D.C. From 1985 until 2002, Dr. Pastor was a professor at Emory University and fellow and founding director of the Latin American Program and the Democracy and Election-Monitoring Initiatives at the Carter Center in Atlanta. He is the author/editor of 16 books on foreign policy and democratization.

Recep Senturk is associate professor of sociology at the Center for Islamic Research (ISAM) in Istanbul and a research fellow at Emory University Law School in Atlanta. His recent publications include *New Sociologies of Religion* (Istanbul, 2004, in Turkish) and *Narrative Social Structure: Anatomy of the Hadith Transmission Network, 610–1505* (Stanford University Press, forthcoming September 2005).